The Observer's Pocket Series

AIRCRAFT

The Observer Books

A POCKET REFERENCE SERIES
COVERING NATURAL HISTORY, TRANSPORT, THE ARTS ETC

The Observer's Book of
AIRCRAFT

COMPILED BY
WILLIAM GREEN

WITH SILHOUETTES BY
DENNIS PUNNETT

DESCRIBING 137 AIRCRAFT
WITH 245 ILLUSTRATIONS

1975 Edition

FREDERICK WARNE & CO LTD
FREDERICK WARNE & CO INC
LONDON · NEW YORK

© FREDERICK WARNE & CO LTD
LONDON, ENGLAND

1975

Twenty-fourth Edition 1975

LIBRARY OF CONGRESS CATALOG CARD NO; 57–4425

ISBN 0 7232 1541 3

Printed in Great Britain

INTRODUCTION TO THE 1975 EDITION

As this, the 24th annual edition, was passed for press, serious economic problems were bedevilling aircraft manufacturer and operator alike, and portents for this year appeared anything but favourable from the aviation viewpoint. Worldwide inflation in labour and raw materials costs, compounded by ever-escalating fuel prices, were seriously affecting the buoyancy of the market for new commercial aircraft and most major western airliners were posed serious financial problems, which, in some cases, were threatening survival. Indeed, such was the climate that no new large western airliner was in prospect and highly promising projects were being shelved or abandoned, one such casualty being the Hawker Siddeley HS.146 short-haul airliner which it had been anticipated would fly towards the end of this year.

Thus, in so far as commercial aircraft are concerned, 1975 holds little promise of vintage class if not completely devoid of civil débutantes. One newcomer, of which much is expected, is de Havilland Canada's Dash-7 STOL transport (page 68), which should have flown by the time these words are read, and another, from the Soviet Union, is the Yak-42, which, designed for operation from restricted airfields, should have flown before the year's end. The Boeing 747SP (page 36), a lower-weight longer-range derivative of the basic Model 747, is expected to appear shortly after mid-year, and at least two interesting light STOL utility transports, the AM-C 111 (page 14) and the Master Porter (page 160), may be expected to appear in Europe during the course of the year.

While the tempo of commercial aircraft development is undeniably slowing, that of military aircraft is continuing apace, and at the time of closing for press, two decisions that could have far-reaching effects on the fighter scene during the closing years of this decade were imminent: the selection of a new fighter by four NATO countries—the Netherlands, Belgium, Denmark and Norway—and the choice by the USAF between the YF-16 (page 86) and YF-17 (page 150) as the basis for its new Air Combat Fighter (ACF). Variable-geometry combat aircraft are beginning to proliferate. In the west both the Panavia MRCA and the Rockwell International B-1 are now flying, while several types are now in service in the east, one of which, the Su-20 (page 198) appears in this edition for the first time.

For those readers unfamiliar with *The Observer's Book of Aircraft*, the *raison d'être* of this annual should perhaps be restated. It is intended to present in compact form each year the new aircraft types and variants of existing types that have appeared during the preceding twelve months or may be expected to appear during the year of currency of the volume. For those aircraft that the reader is most likely to *see*, the companion *Observer's Basic Aircraft Directories* are recommended.

WILLIAM GREEN

AERITALIA (FIAT) G.222

Country of Origin: Italy.

Type: General-purpose military transport.

Power Plant: Two 3 400 shp General Electric T64-P4D turboprops.

Performance: Max. speed, 329 mph (530 km/h) at sea level, 336 mph (540 km/h) at 15,000 ft (4 575 m); normal cruise, 224 mph (360 km/h) at 14,750 ft (4 500 m); range with 11,025-lb (5 000-kg) payload, 1,920 mls (3 250 km), with max. fuel, 3,262 mls (5 250 km); max. initial climb rate, 1,890 ft/min (9,6 m/sec).

Weights: Empty, 32,165 lb (14 590 kg); empty equipped, 33,950 lb (15 400 kg); max. take-off, 58,422 lb (26 500 kg).

Accommodation: Flight crew of three or four and seats for 44 fully-equipped troops or 40 paratroops. Alternative loads include 36 casualty stretchers, two jeep-type vehicles or equivalent freight.

Status: First of two prototypes flown July 18, 1970, followed by second prototype on July 22, 1971. An order for 44 aircraft for the Italian Air Force was placed on July 28, 1972, with first two production aircraft scheduled to fly and be delivered by mid-1975.

Notes: Prototypes powered by CT64-820 turboprops and unpressurised, but the current production model will have uprated T64-P4D turboprops and provision for pressurisation. The G.222 is intended as a successor to some of the Italian Air Force's ageing Fairchild C-119 transports. Current planning calls for the G.222 to equip two squadrons of the Italian Air Force.

AERITALIA (FIAT) G.222

Dimensions: Span, 94 ft 5¾ in (28,80 m); length, 74 ft 5½ in (22,70 m); height, 32 ft 1¾ in (9,80 m); wing area, 970·9 sq ft (90,2 m²).

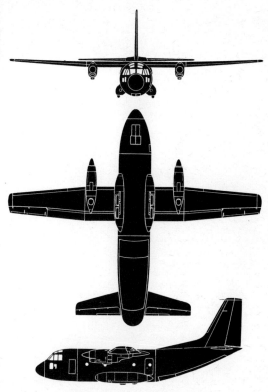

AERO L 39 ALBATROSS

Country of Origin: Czechoslovakia.

Type: Tandem two-seat basic and advanced trainer.

Power Plant: One 3,792 lb (1 720 kg) Walter Titan (Ivchenko AI-25TL) turbofan.

Performance: (At 9,259 lb/4 200 kg) Max. speed, 438 mph (705 km/h) at sea level, 470 mph (757km/h) at 16,405 ft (5 000 m), 457 mph (737 km/h) at 32,810 ft (10 000 m); initial climb, 4,330 ft/min (22 m/sec); time to 16,405 ft (5 000 m), 5 min, to 32,810 ft (10 000 m), 17 min; max. range (fuselage tanks only), 565 mls (910 km).

Weights: Empty equipped, 7,440 lb (3 375 kg); normal loaded, 9,259 lb (4 200 kg); max. take-off, 10,141 lb (4 600 kg).

Armament: (Weapon training) Two wing hard points for gun or rocket pods, or (L 39Z) four wing hard points for ASMs, 16-rocket pods or 20-mm cannon pods.

Status: First of five prototypes flown November 4, 1968, and first of 10 pre-production aircraft flown 1971, with first production deliveries (to Czech and Soviet air forces) commencing 1973.

Notes: Successor to the L 29 Delfin, the L 39 has entered service with the Czech and Soviet air arms, and a light strike variant, the L 39Z, is currently under development and has reportedly been ordered by Iraq, together with the standard training model. The L 39 is expected to be adopted as standard training equipment by all Warsaw Pact countries with the exception of Poland.

AERO L 39 ALBATROSS

Dimensions: Span, 31 ft 0½ in (9,46 m); length, 40 ft 5 in (12,32 m); height, 15 ft 5⅘ in (4,72 m); wing area, 202·36 sq ft (18,8 m²).

AÉROSPATIALE CORVETTE 100

Country of Origin: France.

Type: Light business executive transport.

Power Plant: Two 2,310 lb (1 048 kg) UACL JT15D-4 turbofans.

Performance: Max. cruise at 12,125 lb (5 500 kg), 495 mph (796 km/h) at 29,530 ft (9 000 m), at 13,448 lb (6 100 kg), 483 mph (778 km/h) at 25,000 ft (7 620 m); econ. cruise, 385 mph (620 km/h) at 36,090 ft (11 000 m); max. range on internal fuel, 913 mls (1 470 km) at econ. cruise with reserves for 45 min hold at 5,000 ft (1 520 m), with optional 77 Imp gal (350 l) wingtip tanks, 1,520 mls (2 445 km); max. climb, 3,000 ft/min (15,25 m/sec).

Weights: Basic operating, 8,448 lb (3 832 kg); max. take-off, 13,889 lb (6 300 kg).

Accommodation: Crew of one or two on flight deck plus 4–6 passengers in executive version. Standard arrangements for 8, 10 or 12 passengers and aeromedical arrangement for three stretchers and two medical attendants.

Status: Prototype (SN 600) flown July 16, 1970, followed by first of two pre-series aircraft (SN 601) on December 20, 1972. First of initial production series of five flown November 9, 1973, with approximately a dozen delivered by the beginning of 1975 when a production rate of two per month was planned.

Notes: A projected development of the Corvette 100 is the Corvette 200 with a 6·56-ft (2,0-m) fuselage stretch permitting accommodation of up to 18 passengers. A further projected derivative is the three-engined Corvette 300.

AÉROSPATIALE CORVETTE 100

Dimensions: Span, 42 ft $2\frac{2}{5}$ in (12,87 m), with tip tanks, 45 ft 0 in (13,72 m); length, 45 ft 4 in (13,82 m); height, 13 ft 10 in (4,23 m); wing area, 236·8 sq ft (22,00 m²).

AIRBUS A300B2

Country of Origin: International consortium.

Type: Short- to medium-range commercial transport.

Power Plant: Two 49,000 lb (22 260 kg) General Electric CF6-50A or (from 1975) 51,000 lb (23 133 kg) CF6-50C turbofans.

Performance: Max. cruise, 582 mph (937 km/h) at 25,000 ft (7 620 m); typical high-speed cruise, 570 mph (917 km/h) at 30,000 ft (9 145 m); typical long-range cruise, 526 mph (847 km/h) at 31,000 ft (9 450 m); range with 281 passengers, 1,615 mls (2 600 km), with max. fuel, 2,300 mls (3 700 km).

Weights: Typical operational empty, 186,810 lb (84 740 kg); max. take-off, 302,032 lb (137 000 kg).

Accommodation: Basic flight crew of three and basic arrangement for 281 passengers with high-density arrangement for 345 passengers.

Status: First and second A300Bs (dimensionally to B1 standard) flown October 28, 1972, and February 5, 1973, respectively, with third A300B (to B2 standard) flying on June 28, 1973. First of seven A300B2s (plus nine on option) for Air France delivered May 1974, with deliveries of three (with four on option) to Lufthansa commencing 1975. Nine were produced in 1974, and 30 are scheduled for production in 1975.

Notes: The A300B is being manufactured by an international consortium comprising Aérospatiale (France), Deutsche Airbus (Federal Germany), Hawker Siddeley (UK), CASA (Spain) and Fokker-VFW (Netherlands), the programme being managed by Airbus Industrie. The A300B1 has a 167 ft 2¼ in (50,97 m) fuselage, and the longer-range A300B4 will have a 330,700 lb (150 000 kg) gross weight.

AIRBUS A300B2

Dimensions: Span, 147 ft 1¼ in (44,84 m); length, 175 ft 11 in (53,62 m); height, 54 ft 2 in (16,53 m); wing area, 2,799 sq ft (260,0 m²).

AIR METAL AM-C 111

Country of Origin: Federal Germany.

Type: Light STOL utility transport.

Power Plant: Two 1,120 shp UACL PT6A-45 turboprops.

Performance: (Estimated) Max. cruise, 258 mph (415 km/h) at sea level, 248 mph (400 km/h) at 20,000 ft (6 095 m); range (max. fuel and 1,830-lb/830-kg payload), 1,710 mls (2 750 km), (with 4,409-lb/2 000-kg payload), 620 mls (1 000 km); initial climb, 2,000 ft/min (10,16 m/sec); service ceiling, 25,425 ft (7 750 m).

Weights: Standard empty, 8,000 lb (3 629 kg); max. takeoff, 14,990 lb (6 800 kg).

Accommodation: Flight crew of two and 24 passengers in airline configuration or up to 30 in high-density configuration.

Status: First of two prototypes was scheduled to fly early 1975. Air Metal proposes to build small series of production aircraft as pattern machines and subsequently concentrate on sub-assembly kits for assembly by licensees in various parts of the world.

Notes: AM-C 111 is known as the Series 100 in its initial unpressurised form, the Series 300 differing in having a rear loading ramp, the equivalent pressurised versions being the Series 200 and 400. A projected stretched-fuselage version is the Series 100S.

AIR METAL AM-C 111

Dimensions: Span, 62 ft 4 in (19,00 m); length, 53 ft 0¾ in (16,34 m); height, 21 ft 0 in (6,40 m); wing area, 403·7 sq ft (37,50 m²).

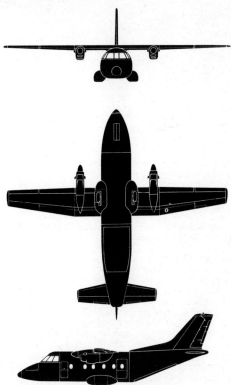

ANTONOV AN-28

Country of Origin: USSR.
Type: Light STOL general-purpose transport and feederliner.
Power Plant: Two 810 shp Isotov TVD-850 turboprops.
Performance: Max. speed, 205 mph (330 km/h); max. continuous cruise, 189 mph (305 km/h); range with max. payload, 560 mls (900 km), with max. fuel, 715 mls (1 150 km); service ceiling, 19,685 ft (6 000 m).
Weights: Empty equipped, 7,716 lb (3 500 kg); normal take-off, 12,346 lb (5 600 kg).
Accommodation: Normal flight crew of two and accommodation for 15 passengers in three-abreast seating (two to starboard and one to port), the seats folding back against the cabin walls when the aircraft is employed in the freighter or mixed passenger/freight roles.
Status: Initial prototype (An-14M) flown September 1969, with initial deliveries (to Aeroflot) anticipated for 1975.
Notes: Essentially a scaled-up, turboprop-powered derivative of the piston-engined An-14, the An-28 was initially referred to as the An-14M (see 1973 edition) and has suffered a somewhat protracted gestation. The An-28 can operate with a full payload (2,865 lb/1 300 kg) under hot-and-high conditions and will be operated over Aeroflot's shortest routes and particularly those currently operated by An-2 biplanes. The An-28 is being proposed for parachute training, geological survey, fire fighting, rescue operations and agricultural tasks.

ANTONOV AN-28

Dimensions: Span, 72 ft 2⅛ in (22,00 m); length, 42 ft 6⅞ in (12,98 m); height, 15 ft 1 in (4,60 m).

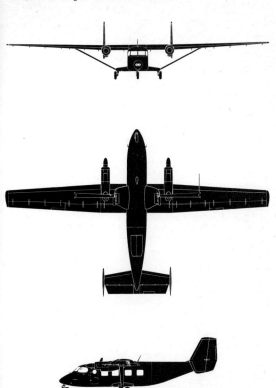

ANTONOV AN-30 (CLANK)

Country of Origin: USSR.

Type: Aerial survey aircraft.

Power Plant: Two 2,820 ehp Ivchenko AI-24T turboprops and one 1,764 lb (800 kg) Tumansky RU-19A-300 auxiliary turbojet.

Performance: Max. speed, 323 mph (520 km/h) at 19,685 ft (6 000 m); normal cruise, 264 mph (425 km/h); initial climb, 1,575 ft/min (8,0 m/sec); service ceiling, 27,230 ft (8 300 m); range, 1,616 mls (2 600 km); endurance, 6 hrs.

Weights: Empty equipped, 32,408 lb (14 700 kg); max. take-off, 50,706 lb (23 000 kg).

Accommodation: Standard crew of seven, including pilot, co-pilot, navigator, engineer and three photographers/ systems operators.

Status: The prototype An-30 initiated its flight test programme mid-1973 and is expected to enter service with Aeroflot during the course of 1975.

Notes: The An-30 is a specialised aerial survey derivative of the An-24RT which, in turn, is a specialised freighter version of the An-24V *Seriiny II* (see 1969 edition) commercial transport. For the primary task of aerial photography for mapmaking, the An-30 is provided with four large survey cameras, and hatches permit the use of laser, thermographic, gravimetric, magnetic and geophysical sensors. The An-30 may also be used for microwave radiometer-survey or mineral prospecting. Equipment includes a computer into which is fed a pre-programmed flight path, the computer subsequently controlling aircraft speed, altitude and course throughout the mission.

ANTONOV AN-30 (CLANK)

Dimensions: Span, 95 ft 9½ in (29,20 m); length, 79 ft 7⅛ in (24,26 m); height, 27 ft 3½ in (8,32 m); wing area, 807·1 sq ft (74,98 m²).

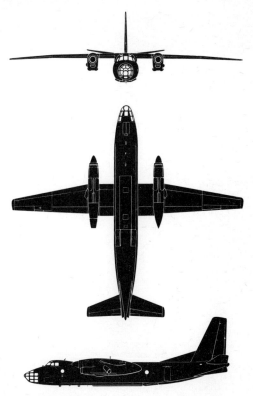

BAC 167 STRIKEMASTER

Country of Origin: United Kingdom.

Type: Side-by-side two-seat basic trainer and light attack and counter-insurgency aircraft.

Power Plant: One 3,410 lb (1 547 kg) Rolls-Royce Viper 535 turbojet.

Performance: Max. speed, 450 mph (724 km/h) at sea level, 472 mph (760 km/h) at 20,000 ft (6 096 m); range at 8,355 lb (3 789 kg), 725 mls (1 166 km), at 10,500 lb (4 762 kg), 1,238 mls (1 992 km), at 11,500 lb (5 216 kg), 1,382 mls (2 224 km); initial climb at 8,355 lb (3 789 kg), 5,250 ft/min (26,67 m/sec); time to 30,000 ft (9 150 m), 8 min 45 sec, to 40,000 ft (12 200 m), 15 min 30 sec.

Weights: Empty equipped, 5,850 lb (2 653 kg); normal take-off (pilot training), 8,355 lb (3 789 kg), (navigational training), 9,143 lb (4 147 kg); max. 11,500 lb (5 216 kg).

Armament: Provision for two 7,62-mm FN machine guns with 550 rpg and eight underwing stores stations for up to 3,000 lb (1 360 kg) of stores.

Status: Prototype Strikemaster flown October 26, 1967, with production deliveries following late 1968. Versions ordered and which differ only in equipment specified include Mk. 80 (Saudi Arabia), Mk. 81 (South Yemen), Mk. 82 (Muscat and Oman), Mk. 83 (Kuwait), Mk. 84 (Singapore), Mk. 87 (Kenya), Mk. 88 (New Zealand) and Mk. 89 (Ecuador). Total of 134 Strikemasters contracted for by beginning of 1975 when limited production was continuing.

Notes: Derivative of the externally similar BAC 145 Jet Provost T. Mk. 5 (see 1971 edition) from which it differs primarily in having a more powerful engine, some local structural strengthening, and additional stores stations.

BAC 167 STRIKEMASTER

Dimensions: Span, 35 ft 4 in (10,77 m); length, 34 ft 0 in (10,36 m); height, 10 ft 2 in (3,10 m); wing area, 213·7 sq ft (19,80 m²).

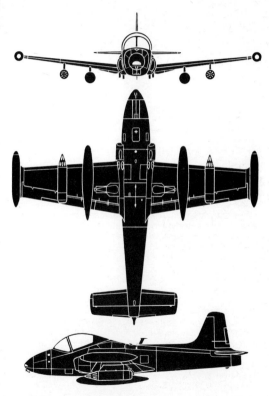

BAC ONE-ELEVEN 475

Country of Origin: United Kingdom.
Type: Short- to medium-range commercial transport.
Power Plant: Two 12,550 lb (5 692 kg) Rolls-Royce Spey 512-14-DW turbofans.
Performance: Max. cruise, 548 mph (882 km/h) at 21,000 ft (6 400 m); econ. cruise, 507 mph (815 km/h) at 25,000 ft (7 620 m); range with reserves for 230 mls (370 km) diversion and 45 min, 2,095 mls (3 370 km), with capacity payload, 1,590 mls (2 560 km); initial climb rate at 345 mph (555 km/h), 2,350 ft/min (11,93 m/sec).
Weights: Basic operational, 51,814 lb (23 502 kg); max. take-off, 92,000 lb (41 730 kg).
Accommodation: Basic flight crew of two and up to 89 passengers. Typical arrangement provides for 16 first- (four-abreast) and 49 tourist-class (five-abreast) passengers.
Status: Aerodynamic prototype of One-Eleven 475 flown August 27, 1970 followed by first production model on April 5, 1971, with certification and first production deliveries following in June. Total of 215 examples of all versions of the One-Eleven ordered by beginning of 1975.
Notes: The One-Eleven 475 combines the standard fuselage of the Series 400 with the redesigned wing and uprated engines of the Series 500 (see 1970 edition), coupling these with a low-pressure undercarriage to permit operation from gravel or low-strength sealed runways. The One-Eleven prototype flew on August 20, 1963, production models including the physically similar Series 200 and 300 with 10,330 lb (4 686 kg) Spey 506s and 11,400 lb (5 170 kg) Spey 511s, the Series 400 modified for US operation, and the Series 500 which is similar to the 475 apart from the fuselage and undercarriage.

BAC ONE-ELEVEN 475

Dimensions: Span, 93 ft 6 in (28,50 m); length, 93 ft 6 in (28,50 m); height, 24 ft 6 in (7,47 m); wing area, 1,031 sq ft (95,78 m²).

BAC-AÉROSPATIALE, CONCORDE

Countries of Origin: United Kingdom and France.
Type: Long-range supersonic commercial transport.
Power Plant: Four 38,050 lb (17 259 kg) reheat Rolls-Royce/SNECMA Olympus 593 Mk. 610 turbojets.
Performance: Max. cruise, 1,450 mph (2 330 km/h) or Mach 2·2 at 54,500 ft (16 000 m); max. range cruise, 1,350 mph (2 170 km/h) or Mach 2·05; max. fuel range with FAR reserves and 17,000-lb (7 710-kg) payload, 4,400 mls (7 080 km); max. payload range, 3,600 mls (5 790 km) at 616 mph (990 km/h) or Mach 0·93 at 30,000 ft (9 100 m), 4,020 mls (6 470 km) at 1,350 mph (2 170 km/h) or Mach 2·05 at 54,500 ft (16 000 m); initial climb, 5,000 ft/min (25,4 m/sec).
Weights: Operational empty, 169,000 lb (76 650 kg); max. take-off, 400,000 lb (181 400 kg).
Accommodation: Normal flight crew of three and economy-class seating for 128 passengers. Alternative high-density arrangement for 144 passengers.
Status: First and second prototypes flown March 2 and April 9, 1969 respectively. First of two pre-production aircraft flew December 17, 1971, the second (illustrated above) flying on January 10, 1973. The first production aircraft was flown on December 6, 1973, and had been joined by one other by the beginning of 1975 when 14 additional Concordes were under construction.
Notes: The Concorde reached Mach 2·0 on November 4, 1970, the prototypes having 34,700 lb (15 740 kg) Olympus 593-3Bs. Orders at the beginning of 1975 comprised five for British Airways and four for Air France, and scheduled in-service date is April 1976.

BAC-AÉROSPATIALE CONCORDE

Dimensions: Span, 84 ft 0 in (25,60 m); length, 203 ft 8¾ in (62,10 m); height, 39 ft 10¼ in (12,15 m); wing area, 3,856 sq ft (358,25 m²).

BEECHCRAFT SUPER KING AIR 200

Country of Origin: USA.
Type: Light business executive transport.
Power Plant: Two 850 shp UACL (Pratt & Whitney) PT6A-41 turboprops.
Performance: Max. cruise, 333 mph (536 km/h) at 12,000 ft (3 655 m), 320 mph (515 km/h) at 25,000 ft (7 620 m); max. range, 1,840 mls (2 961 km) at 27,000 ft (8 230 m) at max. cruise, 2,045 mls (3 290 km) at max. range cruise; initial climb, 2,450 ft/min (12,44 m/sec); service ceiling, 32,300 ft (9 845 m).
Weights: Empty equipped, 7,650 lb (3 470 kg); max. take-off, 12,500 lb (5 670 kg).
Accommodation: Flight crew of two and standard arrangement of six individual seats in main cabin with an optional eight-passenger arrangement. High-density configuration available.
Status: Prototype Super King Air flown October 27, 1972, with second example following on December 15. Customer deliveries commenced March 1974.
Notes: The Super King Air 200 is the fourth aircraft in the King Air range and differs from the King Air A100 (see 1972 edition) primarily in having increased wing span, higher cabin pressure differential, increased fuel tankage, uprated turboprops and a T-tail arrangement. The King Air E90 (see 1973 edition) is basically a more powerful version of the C90 possessing similar turboprops to those of the A100. The C90, E90 and A100 remain in production. Fourteen Super King Air A200s (with 750 hp PT6A-38s) are being delivered to the USAF as C-12As and 20 to the US Army as U-25A Hurons.

BEECHCRAFT SUPER KING AIR 200

Dimensions: Span, 54 ft 6 in (16,60 m); length, 43 ft 9 in (13,16 m); height, 14 ft 11½ in (4,54 m); wing area, 303 sq ft (28,1 m²).

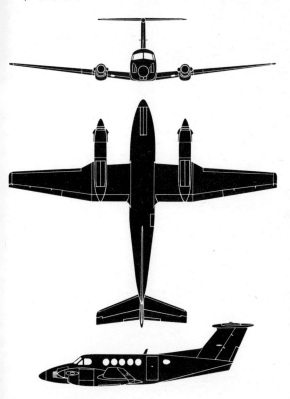

BELLANCA MODEL 8GCBC SCOUT

Country of Origin: USA.

Type: Light cabin monoplane.

Power Plant: One 180 hp Avco Lycoming O-360-C2A four-cylinder horizontally-opposed engine.

Performance: Max. speed, 135 mph (217 km/h) at sea level; max. cruise, 130 mph (209 km/h); range at 75% power, 450 mls (724 km) at 8,000 ft (2 438 m); initial climb, 1,110 ft/min (5,6 m/sec).

Weights: Empty, 1,315 lb (594 kg); max. take-off (normal category), 2,150 lb (975 kg).

Accommodation: Enclosed cabin seating two persons in tandem. Provision for 75 Imp gal (340 l) chemical tank for agricultural role.

Status: A more powerful version of the original Model 7GCBC Scout first announced in December 1970, the Model 8GCBC appeared in 1974 with customer deliveries commencing in May of that year.

Notes: The Model 8GCBC Scout is a utility version of the Model 7KCAB Citabria sporting and aerobatic monoplane originally marketed by Champion Aircraft acquired by Bellanca in 1970. The original Model 7GCBC Scout had a 150 hp Lycoming O-320-A2B engine and, in addition to a more powerful engine, the new version of the Scout differs in having larger vertical tail surfaces, Hoerner wingtips, 27-deg high-lift flaps and a strengthened undercarriage with oversize balloon tyres. Skiis or Edo 2000 floats may replace the wheel undercarriage.

BELLANCA MODEL 8GCBC SCOUT

Dimensions: Span, 36 ft 3¼ in (11,05 m); length, 22 ft 8⅔ in (6,92 m); height, 7 ft 8½ in (2,35 m); wing area, 180 sq ft (16,72 m²).

BELLANCA SUPER VIKING 300A

Country of Origin: USA.

Type: Light cabin monoplane.

Power Plant: (Model 17-30A) One 300 hp Continental IO-520K six-cylinder horizontally-opposed engine.

Performance: (Model 17-30A) Max. speed, 226 mph (363 km/h); cruise at 75% power, 187 mph (301 km/h); max. range (standard fuel), 870 mls (1 400 km); initial climb, 1,170 ft/min (5,93 m/sec); service ceiling, 17,000 ft (5 180 m).

Weights: (Model 17-30A) Empty, 2,191 lb (994 kg); max. take-off, 3,325 lb (1 508 kg).

Accommodation: Four seats in pairs. Dual controls standard.

Status: The Model 17 Super Viking 300A is a progressive development of the Model 17 Viking introduced in 1966, and is currently manufactured as the Model 17-30A (described above), the Model 17-31A with a 300 hp Avco Lycoming IO-540-K1E5 engine and as the Model 17-31ATC with the Lycoming engine and two Rajay superchargers. Production of all versions of the Super Viking averaged 12 per month during 1974.

Notes: The Super Viking stems from the original Bellanca Model 14 Cruiser of 1937 which re-entered production after WW II as the Cruisemaster, introducing a tricycle undercarriage with the Model 14-19-3 which, with redesigned tail and increased power, became the Model 17.

BELLANCA SUPER VIKING 300A

Dimensions: Span, 34 ft 2 in (10,41 m); length, 26 ft 3 in (7,99 m); height, 7 ft 4 in (2,24 m); wing area, 161·5 sq ft (15,00 m²).

BOEING MODEL 727-200

Country of Origin: USA.

Type: Short- to medium-range commercial transport.

Power Plant: Three 14,500 lb (6 577 kg) Pratt & Whitney JT8D-9 turbofans (with 15,000 lb/6 804 kg JT8D-11s or 15,500 lb/7 030 kg JT8D-15s as options).

Performance: Max. speed, 621 mph (999 km/h) at 20,500 ft (6 250 m); max. cruise, 599 mph (964 km/h) at 24,700 ft (7 530 m); econ. cruise, 570 mph (917 km/h) at 30,000 m (9 145 m); range with 26,400-lb (11 974-kg) payload and normal reserves, 2,850 mls (4 585 km), with max. payload (41,000 lb/18 597 kg), 1,845 mls (2 970 km).

Weights: Operational empty (basic), 97,525 lb (44 235 kg), (typical), 99,000 lb (44 905 kg); max. take-off, 208,000 lb (94 347 kg).

Accommodation: Crew of three on flight deck and six-abreast seating for 163 passengers in basic arrangement with max. seating for 189 passengers.

Status: First Model 727-100 flown February 9, 1963, with first delivery (to United) following October 29, 1963. Model 727-200 flown July 27, 1967, with first delivery (to North-east) on December 11, 1967. Deliveries from mid-1972 have been of the so-called "Advanced 727-200" (to which specification refers and illustrations apply) and a total of approximately 1,200 Model 727s ordered by 1975.

Notes: The Model 727-200 is a "stretched" version of the 727-100 (see 1972 edition). Deliveries of the "Advanced 727" with JT8D-17 engines of 16,000 lb (7 257 kg), permitting an increase of 3,500 lb (1 587 kg) in payload, began (to Mexicana) in June 1974. The proposed Model 727-300 has a 15-ft (4,57-m) longer fuselage, modified wing with Krueger flaps and extended wingtips, and a gross weight in excess of 210,000 lb (95 255 kg).

BOEING MODEL 727-200

Dimensions: Span, 108 ft 0 in (32,92 m); length, 153 ft 2 in (46,69 m); height, 34 ft 0 in (10,36 m); wing area, 1,700 sq ft (157,9 m²).

BOEING MODEL 747B

Country of Origin: USA.

Type: Long-range large-capacity commercial transport.

Power Plant: Four 47,000 lb (21 320 kg) Pratt & Whitney JT9D-7W turbofans.

Performance: Max. speed at 600,000 lb (272 155 kg), 608 mph (978 km/h) at 30,000 ft (9 150 m); long-range cruise, 589 mph (948 km/h) at 35,000 ft (10 670 m); range with max. fuel and FAR reserves, 7,080 mls (11 395 km), with 79,618-lb (36 114-kg) payload, 6,620 mls (10 650 km); cruise ceiling, 45,000 ft (13 715 m).

Weights: Operational empty, 361,216 lb (163 844 kg); max. take-off, 775,000 lb (351 540 kg).

Accommodation: Normal flight crew of three and basic accommodation for 66 first-class and 308 economy-class passengers. Alternative layouts for 447 or 490 economy-class passengers nine- and 10-abreast respectively.

Status: First Model 747-100 flown on February 9, 1969, and first commercial services (by Pan American) inaugurated January 22, 1970. The first Model 747-200 (747B), the 88th aircraft off the assembly line, flown October 11, 1970.

Notes: Principal versions are the -100 and -200 series, the latter having greater fuel capacity and increased maximum take-off weight, convertible passenger/cargo and all-cargo versions of the -200 series (alias Model 747B) being designated 747C and 747F. The first production example of the latter flew on November 30, 1971. Deliveries of the Model 747SR, a short-range version of the 747-100 (to Japan Air Lines), began September 1973. The 747-300, flown on June 26, 1973, has 51,000 lb (23 133 kg) General Electric CF6-50D engines.

BOEING MODEL 747B

Dimensions: Span, 195 ft 8 in (59,64 m); length, 231 ft 4 in (70,51 m); height, 63 ft 5 in (19,33 m); wing area, 5,685 sq ft (528,15 m²).

BOEING MODEL 747SP

Country of Origin: USA.

Type: Long-range large-capacity commercial transport.

Power Plant: Four 46,150 lb (20 933 kg) Pratt & Whitney JT9D-7A turbofans.

Performance: (Estimated at 600,000 lb/272 160 kg) Long-range cruise, 580 mph (933 km/h) or M=0·88 at 36,000 ft (10 975 m), 568 mph (914 km/h) or M=0·86 at 38,500 ft (11 735 m); max. range (288 passengers and baggage), 6,450 mls (10 380 km) at long-range cruise at 37,000–41,000 ft (11 280–12 500 m), (zero payload), 8,320 mls (13 390 km).

Weights: Operational empty, 315,000 lb (140 878 kg); max. take-off, 650,000 lb (294 835 kg).

Accommodation: Flight crew of three and typical mixed-class accommodation for 288 passengers (including 16 in top deck cabin aft of flight deck. Typical all-economy high-density arrangement for 360 passengers with maximum capacity of 412 in 10-abreast seating.

Status: First Model 747SP scheduled to fly July 1975, with first delivery (to Pan American) in February 1976. In addition to the order from Pan American (for five aircraft), the Model 747SP has been ordered by Japan Air Lines and Iran Air.

Notes: The Model 747SP has been designed primarily for operation over long-range routes where traffic densities are insufficient to support the standard Model 747 (see pages 34–35), and has some 90 per cent commonality with the original version. The Model 747SP has a 48 ft 4 in (14,70 m) shorter fuselage, taller vertical surfaces with a double-hinged rudder and new trailing-edge flaps.

BOEING MODEL 747SP

Dimensions: Span, 195 ft 8 in (59,64 m); length, 176 ft 8½ in (53,86 m); height, 65 ft 6 in (19,96 m); wing area, 5,685 sq ft (528,15 m²).

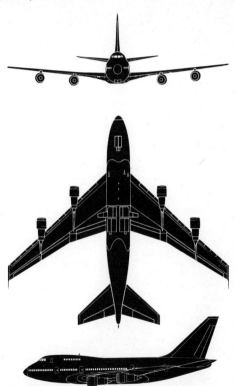

BOEING E-3A

Country of Origin: USA.

Type: Airborne warning and control system aircraft.

Power Plant: Four 21,000 lb (9 525 kg) Pratt & Whitney TF33-P-7 turbofans.

Performance: No details have been released for publication, but max. and econ. cruise speeds are likely to be generally similar to those of the equivalent commercial Model 707-320B (i.e., 627 mph/1 010 km/h and 550 mph/886 km/h respectively). Mission requirement is for 7-hr search at 29,000 ft (8 840 m) at 1,150 mls (1 850 km) from base. Unrefuelled endurance, 11·5 hrs.

Weights: Approx. max. take-off, 330,000 lb (149 685 kg).

Accommodation: The E-3A will carry an operational crew of 17 which may be increased according to mission. The compliment comprises a flight crew of four, a four-man systems maintenance team, a battle commander and an eight-man air defence operations team.

Status: First of two EC-137D development aircraft flown February 9, 1972. Three pre-production examples of the operational derivative, the E-3A (one using EC-137D airframe) are being produced, with the first (the EC-137D conversion) having been scheduled for trials in February 1975, and the second and third being delivered during the last quarter of 1975. Deliveries commencing in spring of 1976 of anticipated total of 31 production E-3As.

Notes: As part of a programme for the development of a new AWACS (Airborne Warning And Control System) aircraft for operation by the USAF from the mid 'seventies, two Boeing 707-320B transports have been modified as EC-137D testbeds. These were employed during 1972 for competitive evaluation of the competing Hughes and Westinghouse radars, the latter having been selected as winning contender.

BOEING E-3A

Dimensions: Span, 145 ft 9 in (44,42 m); length, 152 ft 11 in (46,61 m); height, 42 ft 5 in (12,93 m); wing area, 3,050 sq ft (283,4 m²).

BOEING T-43A

Country of Origin: USA.
Type: Military navigational trainer.
Power Plant: Two 14,500 lb (6 577 kg) Pratt & Whitney JT8D-9 turbofans.
Performance: Max. speed, 576 mph (927 km/h) at 23,000 ft (7 010 m); max. range, 3,225 mls (5 190 km); training mission endurance, 1 hr 30 min at low altitude, 4 hr 40 min at long-range cruise at 35,000 ft (10 668 m), 5 hr 30 min at max. time cruise at 30,000 ft (9 144 m).
Weights: Zero fuel, 68,454 lb (31 050 kg); design mission gross, 106,167 lb (48 157 kg); max. take-off, 115,500 lb (52 390 kg).
Accommodation: Flight crew of two. Cabin provides three instructor stations, 12 student stations and four navigator proficiency stations.
Status: First of 19 T-43As ordered by USAF flown on April 10, 1973 with completion of order July 1974.
Notes: Ordered in May 1971 as a successor to the piston-engined Convair T-29 at the USAF Air Training Command's Navigation Training School at Mather, the T-43A is basically a modified Model 737-200 commercial transport (see 1973 edition) airframe with several new features specified by the USAF, including an aft body fuselage fuel tank in the space normally occupied by the rear underfloor baggage hold and provision for a further fuselage tank. The T-43A incorporates all the improvements that have been engineered for the so-called "Advanced 737-200", which standard was introduced from May 1971. A total of 415 examples of the commercial transport had been ordered by November 1974 with some 380 delivered.

BOEING T-43A

Dimensions: Span, 93 ft 0 in (28,35 m); length, 100 ft 0 in (30,48 m); height, 37 ft 0 in (11,28 m); wing area, 980 sq ft (91,05 m²).

BRITTEN-NORMAN BN-2A-8S ISLANDER

Country of Origin: United Kingdom.

Type: Light utility transport.

Power Plant: Two 260 hp Lycoming O-540-E4C5 six-cylinder horizontally-opposed engines.

Performance: Max. speed, 170 mph (273 km/h) at sea level; cruise at 75% power, 160 mph (257 km/h) at 7,000 ft (2 140 m), at 67% power, 158 mph (253 km/h) at 9,000 ft (2 750 m), at 59% power, 154 mph (248 km/h) at 13,000 ft (3 960 m); range with standard fuel, 717 mls (1 154 km) at 160 mph (257 km/h), 870 mls (1 400 km) at 154 mph (248 km/h), tip tanks, 1,040 mls (1 674 km) at 160 mph (257 km/h), 1,263 mls (2 035 km) at 154 mph (248 km/h).

Weights: Empty equipped, 3,675 lb (1 667 kg); max. take-off, 6,600 lb (2 993 kg).

Accommodation: Flight crew of one or two and up to 10 passengers on pairs of bench-type seats.

Status: Prototype flown June 12, 1965, followed by first production aircraft on August 20, 1966. More than 650 ordered by beginning of 1975. Production transferred to Fairey SA in Belgium during 1973, the first Belgian-built example being delivered in December of that year, and 215 airframes being manufactured under contract by IRMA in Rumania. Eighty Islanders to be assembled (20) and part-manufactured (60) in the Philippines.

Notes: The BN-2A-8S features a 45·5-in (1,15-m) longer nose to provide increased baggage space, an additional cabin window each side at the rear, and provision for an additional seat row. These changes, indicated by the suffix "S" (for Stretched), are being offered as customer options. A military multi-role version of the Islander is known as the Defender.

BRITTEN-NORMAN BN-2A-8S ISLANDER

Dimensions: Span, 49 ft 0 in (14,94 m); length, 39 ft 5¼ in (12,02 m); height, 13 ft 8 in (4,16 m); wing area, 325 sq ft (30,2 m²).

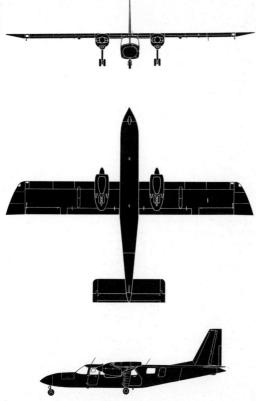

BRITTEN-NORMAN BN-2A MK III TRISLANDER

Country of Origin: United Kingdom.
Type: Light utility transport and feederliner.
Power Plant: Three 260 hp Lycoming O-540-E4C5 six-cylinder horizontally-opposed engines.
Performance: Max. speed, 183 mph (294 km/h) at sea level; cruise at 75% power, 176 mph (283 km/h) at 6,500 ft (1 980 m), at 67% power, 175 mph (282 km/h) at 9,000 ft (2 750 m); range with max. payload, 160 mls (257 m) at 170 mph (274 km/h), with 2,400-lb (1 089-kg) payload, 700 mls (1 127 km) at 175 mph (282 km/h).
Weights: Empty equipped, 5,700 lb (2 585 kg); max. take-off, 10,000 lb (4 536 kg).
Accommodation: Flight crew of one or two, and 16–17 passengers in pairs on bench-type seats.
Status: Prototype flown September 11, 1970, with production prototype flying on March 6, 1971. First production Trislander flown April 29, 1971, and first delivery (to Aurigny) following on June 29, 1971. Trislander production was transferred to Fairey SA at Gosselies, Belgium, late in 1972, and deliveries from the new line began early 1974. Some 40 Trislanders had been ordered by the beginning of 1975, approximately half of these having been delivered.
Notes: The Trislander is a derivative of the Islander (see pages 42–43) with which it has 75% commonality. The wingtip auxiliary fuel tanks optional on the Islander have been standardised for the Trislander, and the only significant differences between the two aircraft are the extra 7 ft 6 in (2,29 m) section ahead of the wing and the strengthened fin structure carrying the third engine. An extended nose version (illustrated above) flew on August 18, 1974.

BRITTEN-NORMAN BN-2A MK III TRISLANDER

Dimensions: Span, 53 ft 0 in (16,15 m); length, 43 ft 9 in (13,33 m); height, 14 ft 2 in (4,32 m); wing area, 337 sq ft (31,25 m²).

CASA C.212 AVIOCAR

Country of Origin: Spain.

Type: STOL utility transport, navigational trainer and photographic survey aircraft.

Power Plant: Two 776 eshp (715 shp) Garrett-AiResearch TPE 331-5-251C turboprops.

Performance: (At 13,889 lb/6 300 kg) Max. cruise, 243 mph (391 km/h) at 12,000 ft (3 658 m), 238 mph (383 km/h) at 5,000 ft (1 524 m); initial climb, 1,724 ft/min (8,76 m/sec); service ceiling, 24,605 ft (7 500 m); range with max. payload and reserves (30 min hold at 5,000 ft/ 1 524 m plus 5% take-off weight), 205 mls (330 km) at 12,500 ft (3 810 m), with max. fuel and similar reserves, 1,197 mls (1 927 km).

Weights: Empty equipped, 8,045 lb (3 650 kg); max. take-off, 13,889 lb (6 300 kg); max. payload, 4,409 lb (2 000 kg).

Accommodation: Flight crew of two and 18 passengers in commercial configuration. Ten casualty stretchers and three sitting casualties or medical attendants in ambulance configuration. Provision for up to 15 paratroops and jumpmaster or 4,409 lb (2 000 kg) of cargo.

Status: Two prototypes flown March 26 and October 23, 1971, with first of 12 pre-production examples following November 17, 1972. Initial production batch of 32 for Spanish Air Force with deliveries commencing early 1974. A further 28 have been ordered by the Portuguese Air Force.

Notes: Of pre-production series, eight have been delivered to Air Force (six for photo survey and two as navigational trainers), and of initial production batch 29 are cargo-paratroop transports and three are navigational trainers.

46

CASA C.212 AVIOCAR

Dimensions: Span, 62 ft 4 in (19,00 m); length, 49 ft 10$\frac{1}{2}$ in (15,20 m); height, 20 ft 8$\frac{3}{4}$ in (6,32 m); wing area, 430·556 sq ft (40,0 m²).

CESSNA CITATION SERIES 500

Country of Origin: USA.

Type: Light business executive transport.

Power Plant: Two 2,200 lb (1 000 kg) UACL JT15D-1 turbofans.

Performance: Max. speed, 402 mph (647 km/h) at 26,400 ft (8 046 m); max. cruise, 400 mph (644 km/h) at 25,400 ft (7 740 m); range with eight persons and 45 min reserves at 90% cruise thrust, 1,397 mls (2 248 km), with two persons and same reserves at 90% cruise thrust, 1,502 mls (2 417 km); initial climb, 2,900 ft/min (14,7 m/sec); service ceiling, 38,400 ft (11 704 m).

Weights: Empty 6,390 lb (2 898 kg); max. take-off, 11,500 lb (5 217 kg).

Accommodation: Crew of two on separate flight deck and alternative arrangements for five or six passengers in main cabin.

Status: First of two prototypes flown on September 15, 1969, and first production Citation flown in May 1971. Customer deliveries began in October 1971. Deliveries averaged six per month during 1974, and approximately 230 had been delivered by the beginning of 1975.

Notes: The Citation places emphasis on short-field performance, enabling the aircraft to use some 2,300 US airfields. From early 1975, operational ceiling is being increased from 35,000 to 41,000 ft (10 670 to 12 495 m) and range with reserves is being increased to some 1,500 mls (2 414 km).

CESSNA CITATION SERIES 500

Dimensions: Span, 43 ft 8½ in (13,32 m); length, 43 ft 6 in (13,26 m); height, 14 ft 3¾ in (4,36 m); wing area, 260 sq ft (24,15 m²).

DASSAULT-BREGUET FALCON 10

Country of Origin: France.
Type: Light business executive transport.
Power Plant: Two 3,230 lb (1 465 kg) Garrett-AiResearch TFE-731-2 turbofans.
Performance: Max. cruise, 567 mph (912 km/h) at 30,000 ft (9 145 m), 495 mph (796 km/h) or Mach 0·75 at 45,000 ft (13 716 m); range with four passengers and 45 min reserves, 2,070 mls (3 330 km) at 45,000 ft (13 716 m), 1,495 mls (2 405 km) at max. cruise at 30,000 ft (9 145 m).
Weights: Empty equipped, 10,475 lb (4 750 kg); max. take-off, 18,298 lb (8 300 kg).
Accommodation: Flight crew of two with provision for third crew member on jump seat. Executive version for four passengers with alternative arrangement for seven passengers.
Status: First of three prototypes flown December 1, 1970, followed by second on October 15, 1971, and third on October 16, 1972. The first production Falcon 10 was flown on April 30, 1973, and production deliveries began during November of that year, output being two per month at the beginning of 1975 when some 70 aircraft had been delivered or were on order.
Notes: The Falcon 10 (also known as the Mystère 10) is basically a scaled-down version of the Falcon 20 (see 1974 edition), and at a later stage in development it is proposed to offer the 2,980 lb (1 350 kg) Turboméca-SNECMA Larzac turbofan as an alternative power plant, the second prototype commencing trials during 1973 with a Larzac in its starboard engine nacelle. The Falcon 10 is being offered to the *Armée de l'Air* as a military crew trainer and liaison aircraft, and two examples have been ordered for test and evaluation purposes.

DASSAULT-BREGUET FALCON 10

Dimensions: 42 ft 11 in (13,08 m); length, 45 ft 5$\frac{3}{4}$ in (13,86 m); height, 15 ft 1 in (4,61 m); wing area, 259·4 sq ft 24,1 m^2).

DASSAULT-BREGUET FALCON 30

Country of Origin: France.
Type: Third-level airliner.
Power Plant: Two 6,063 lb (2 750 kg) Avco-Lycoming ALF-502D turbofans.
Performance: (Estimated) Max. cruise, 509 mph (820 km/h) at 25,000 ft (7 620 m); econ. cruise, 441 mph (710 km/h) at 35,000 ft (10 670 m); range with max. payload (7,495 lb/3 400 kg), 870 mls (1 400 km).
Weights: Empty equipped, 21,825 lb (9 900 kg); max. take-off, 35,275 lb (16 000 kg).
Accommodation: Normal flight crew of two and standard accommodation for 30 passengers in three-abreast seating or (Mystère 40) 40 passengers in a four-abreast arrangement.
Status: First of two prototypes flown May 11, 1973, with development continuing at the beginning of 1975.
Notes: The Falcon 30 has been evolved via an earlier project (Falcon 20-T) which was to have featured a smaller diameter fuselage which has been utilised by the prototype Falcon 30. A larger-diameter fuselage is featured by the proposed production model. A three-engined derivative, the Falcon 50, is described and illustrated on pages 54–55. The future of the Falcon 30/Mystère 40 was uncertain at the time of closing for press and the prototype may be utilised primarily as a development vehicle for the Falcon 50.

DASSAULT-BREGUET FALCON 30

Dimensions: Span, 59 ft 1½ in (18,03 m); length, 64 ft 11 in (19,77 m); height, 19 ft 10 in (6,05 m); wing area, 530 sq ft (49,0 m²).

DASSAULT-BREGUET FALCON 50

Country of Origin: France.
Type: Light business executive transport.
Power Plant: Three 3,700 lb (1 678 kg) Garrett-AiResearch TFE 731-3 turbofans.
Performance: (Estimated) Max. cruise, 541 mph (870 km/h); range cruise, 497 mph (800 km/h); range (10 passengers and reserves for 173 mls/278 km diversion and 45 min hold), 2,983 mls (4 800 km) at range cruise, 2,175 mls (3 500 km) at max. cruise.
Weights: Empty equipped, 19,180 lb (8 700 kg); max. take-off, 36,375 lb (16 500 kg).
Accommodation: Flight crew of two and standard business executive arrangement for 8–10 passengers. Up to 14 passengers may be accommodated in high-density arrangement for third level and air taxi operations.
Status: Prototype scheduled to fly during November 1975 with second in October 1976, and first production deliveries anticipated for mid-1977.
Notes: The Falcon 50 is basically a Falcon 20 Series F fuselage, wing and horizontal tail (see 1974 edition) married to revised vertical tail surfaces fairing in to a dorsally-mounted engine and a revised and lengthened tail cone. The wing is located farther aft in relation to the centre fuselage, an additional fuel tank is provided between the cabin and the rear baggage compartment, and the undercarriage, while similar to that of the Falcon 20, has been strengthened to cater for higher all-up weights.

DASSAULT-BREGUET FALCON 50

Dimensions: Span, 53 ft 6½ in (16,32 m); length, 64 ft 5¼ in (19,64 m); height, 21 ft 2½ in (6,46 m); wing area, 441·32 sq ft (41,0 m²).

DASSAULT-BREGUET MIRAGE 5

Country of Origin: France.
Type: Single-seat ground attack fighter.
Power Plant: One 9,436 lb (4 280 kg) dry and 13,670 lb (6 200 kg) reheat SNECMA Atar 9C turbojet.
Performance: Max. speed (clean), 835 mph (1 335 km/h) or Mach 1·1 at sea level, 1,386 mph (2 230 km/h) or Mach 2·1 at 39,370 ft (12 000 m); cruise, 594 mph (956 km/h) at 36,090 ft (11 000 m); combat radius with 2,000-lb (907-kg) bomb load (hi-lo-hi profile), 805 mls (1 300 km), (lo-lo-lo profile), 400 mls (650 km); time to 36,090 ft (11 000 m) at Mach 0·9, 3 min, to 49,210 ft (15 000 m) at Mach 1·8, 6 min 50 sec.
Weights: Empty equipped, 14,550 lb (6 600 kg); max. loaded, 29,760 lb (13 500 kg).
Armament: Two 30-mm DEFA 5-52 cannon with 125 rpg and seven external ordnance stations. Maximum external load (ordnance and fuel), 9,260 lb (4 200 kg).
Status: Prototype flown May 19, 1967, and first deliveries (to Peru) following May 1968. Assembly (for Belgian Air Force) completed in Belgium by SABCA late 1972. Deliveries to Pakistan, Saudi Arabia and Zaïre continuing 1975.
Notes: The Mirage 5 is an export version of the Mirage IIIE (see 1967 edition) optimised for the ground attack role and featuring simplified avionics. Orders fulfilled or in process of fulfilment at beginning of 1975 included 30 (including two two-seaters) for Pakistan, 15 for Peru (including two two-seaters), 14 for Colombia (plus four two-seat Mirage IIIs), 106 for Belgium (including 16 two-seaters and 63 for tac-recce role), 110 for Libya (including 10 two-seaters), six for Venezuela (including two two-seaters), 14 for Abu Dhabi (including two two-seaters), and 50 for the *Armée de l'Air.*

DASSAULT-BREGUET MIRAGE 5

Dimensions: Span, 26 ft 11½ in (8,22 m); length, 51 ft 0¼ in (15,55 m); height, 13 ft 11½ in (4,25 m); wing area, 375·12 sq ft (34,85 m²).

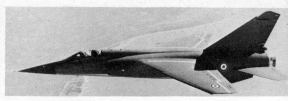

DASSAULT-BREGUET MIRAGE F1

Country of Origin: France.

Type: Single-seat multi-purpose fighter.

Power Plant: One 11,023 lb (5 000 kg) dry and 15,873 lb (7 200 kg) reheat SNECMA Atar 9K-50 turbojet.

Performance: Max. speed (clean), 915 mph (1 472 km/h) or Mach 1·2 at sea level, 1,450 mph (2 335 km/h) or Mach 2·2 at 39,370 ft (12 000 m); range cruise, 550 mph (885 km/h) at 29,530 ft (9 000 m); range with max. external fuel, 2,050 mls (3 300 km), with max. external combat load of 8,818 lb (4 000 kg), 560 mls (900 km), with external combat load of 4,410 lb (2 000 kg), 1,430 mls (2 300 km); service ceiling, 65,600 ft (20 000 m).

Weights: Empty, 16,314 lb (7 400 kg); loaded (clean), 24,030 lb (10 900 kg); max. take-off, 32,850 lb (14 900 kg).

Armament: Two 30-mm DEFA cannon and (intercept) 1-3 Matra 530 Magic and two AIM-9 Sidewinder AAMs.

Status: First of four prototypes flown December 23, 1966. First of 105 ordered for *Armée de l'Air* flown February 15, 1973. Production rate of four—five per month at beginning of 1975. Licence manufacture is to be undertaken in South Africa with deliveries commencing 1977.

Notes: Initial model for *Armée de l'Air* intended primarily for high-altitude intercept role. Proposed versions include F1A for day ground attack role, the F1B two-seat trainer, the F1C interceptor and the 18,740 lb (8 500 kg) with reheat M53-powered multi-role F1E version, the last-mentioned having been scheduled to fly in December 1974. Fifteen Mirage F1s have been ordered by Spain (which country has an option on 18 more), 40 by Greece and 20 by Kuwait, and delivery of 16 Mirage F1CZ interceptors to South Africa began late 1974; these are to be followed by 32 Mirage F1AZ ground attack fighters.

DASSAULT-BREGUET MIRAGE F1

Dimensions: Span, 27 ft $6\frac{3}{4}$ in (8,40 m); length, 49 ft $2\frac{1}{2}$ in (15,00 m); height, 14 ft 9 in (4,50 m); wing area, 269·098 sq ft (25 m²).

DASSAULT-BREGUET SUPER ÉTENDARD

Country of Origin: France.

Type: Single-seat shipboard strike fighter.

Power Plant: One 10,912 lb (4 950 kg) SNECMA Atar 8K-50 turbojet.

Performance: (Estimated) Max. speed (clean), 695 mph (1 118 km/h) or Mach 1·05 at 36,000 ft (11 000 m), 708 mph (1 139 km/h) or Mach 0·93 at sea level; tactical radius (internal fuel), 210 mls (338 km) at sea level, 520 mls (837 km) at 42,650 ft (13 000 m); initial climb, 20,000 ft/min (101,6 m/sec).

Weights: (Estimated) Empty equipped, 14,000 lb (6 350 kg); max. take-off, 24,500 lb (11 113 kg).

Armament: Two 30-mm DEFA cannon in forward fuselage and five external stores stations (one under fuselage and four under wings) for up to approximately 4,000 lb (1 815 kg) of ordnance.

Status: Super Étendard prototype (modified Étendard IVM airframe) commenced its test programme on October 28, 1974. One hundred Super Étendards ordered August 1973 for *Aéronavale* with deliveries to commence 1976.

Notes: More powerful derivative of Étendard IVM (see 1965 edition) with new avionics and some 90 per cent identical structure to that of earlier aircraft. Air-to-surface ordnance planned for use by the Super Étendard includes the AM-39 anti-shipping missile. When it enters service in 1977, the Super Étendard will be the only combat aircraft type aboard the carriers *Foch* and *Clémenceau*.

DASSAULT-BREGUET SUPER ÉTENDARD

Dimensions: Span, 31 ft 6 in (9,60 m); length, 47 ft 3 in (14,40 m); height 14 ft 2 in (4,30 m); wing area, 305·7 sq ft (28,4 m²).

DASSAULT-BREGUET/DORNIER
ALPHA JET

Countries of Origin: France and Federal Germany.
Type: Two-seat advanced trainer and light tactical aircraft.
Power Plant: Two 2,975 lb (1 350 kg) SNECMA-Turbo-méca Larzac 04 turbofans.
Performance: Max. speed, 626 mph (991 km/h) at sea level, 560 mph (901 km/h) at 40,000 ft (12 190 m) or Mach 0·85; radius of action (hi-lo-hi), 390 mls (630 km); max. fuel endurance, 2 hrs at sea level, 3 hrs at 32,810 ft (10 000 m); ferry range (max. external fuel), 1,900 mls (3 057 km); initial climb, 11,800 ft/min (59 m/sec); service ceiling, 45,000 ft (13 700 m).
Weights: Normal take-off (trainer), 10,780 lb (4 890 kg), (close support), 15,340 lb (7 000 kg).
Armament: Provision for external gun pod with 30-mm DEFA 533 cannon and 150 rounds. Close support version has four wing strong points, inboard points being stressed for loads up to 1,250 lb (570 kg) each and outboard points for loads up to 630 lb (285 kg) each.
Status: First of four prototypes flown on October 26, 1973, with last flying on October 11, 1974. Planned production of approx. 200 each for *Armée de l'Air* and *Luftwaffe* with deliveries commencing late 1976. Thirty-three ordered by Belgium with deliveries commencing mid-1977.
Notes: The Alpha Jet is to have two final assembly lines (Toulouse and Munich) and will serve with the *Armée de l'Air* in the training role and for close support with the *Luftwaffe*.

DASSAULT-BREGUET/DORNIER ALPHA JET

Dimensions: Span, 29 ft 11 in (9,11 m); length, 40 ft 3 in (12,29 m); height, 13 ft 9 in (4,19 m); wing area, 188 sq ft (17,50 m²).

DE HAVILLAND CANADA DHC-5D
BUFFALO

Country of Origin: Canada.

Type: STOL military tactical transport.

Power Plant: Two 3,095 shp General Electric CT64-820-4 turboprops.

Performance: Max. cruise, 288 mph (463 km/h) at 40,000 lb (18 144 kg), 261 mph (420 km/h) at 47,000 lb (21 319 kg) at 10,000 ft (3 048 m); range (with 12,200 lb/5 534 kg payload), 403 mls (648 km) for assault STOL mission, (with 18,000 lb/8 165 kg payload), 691 mls (1 112 km) for transport STOL mission; max. range, 2,038 mls (3 280 km); initial climb (at 41,000 lb/18 597 kg), 2,200 ft/min (11,17 m/sec), (at 47,000 lb/21 319 kg), 1,720 ft/min (8,65 m/sec); service ceiling, 31,500 ft (9 600 m).

Weights: Empty operational, 24,800 lb (11 249 kg); max. take-off (assault STOL), 41,000 lb (18 597 kg), (transport STOL), 49,200 lb (22 317 kg).

Accommodation: Flight crew of three and 41 fully-equipped troops, 24 litter patients plus six medical attendants and seated casualties, or 18,000 lb (8 165 kg) of cargo.

Status: First aircraft flown April 9, 1964, and production totalling 59 completed in 1972. Reinstated in production (in DHC-5D version) in 1974 against orders from three customers for 15 aircraft with deliveries commencing 1975.

Notes: The DHC-5D offers increased payload by comparison with original DHC-5 (see 1972 edition), has greater fuel capacity and engines developing full take-off power at higher temperatures and altitudes.

DE HAVILLAND CANADA DHC-5D BUFFALO

Dimensions: Span, 96 ft 0 in (29,26 m); length, 79 ft 0 in (24,08 m); height, 28 ft 8 in (8,73 m); wing area, 945 sq ft (87,8 m²).

DE HAVILLAND CANADA DHC-6
TWIN OTTER SERIES 300

Country of Origin: Canada.

Type: STOL utility transport and feederliner.

Power Plant: Two 652 eshp UACL PT6A-27 turboprops.

Performance: Max. cruise, 210 mph (338 km/h) at 10,000 ft (3 050 m); range at max. cruise with 3,250-lb (1 474-kg) payload, 745 mls (1 198 km), with 14 passengers and 45 min reserves, 780 mls (1 255 km); initial climb at 12,500 lb (5 670 kg), 1,600 ft/min (8,1 m/sec); service ceiling, 26,700 ft (8 138 m).

Weights: Basic operational (including pilot), 7,000 lb (3 180 kg); max. take-off, 12,500 lb (5 670 kg).

Accommodation: Flight crew of one or two and accommodation for up to 20 passengers in basic commuter arrangement. Optional commuter layouts for 18 or 19 passengers, and 13–20-passenger utility version.

Status: First of five (Series 100) pre-production aircraft flown May 20, 1965. Series 100 superseded by Series 200 (see 1969 edition) in April 1968, the latter being joined by the Series 300 with the 231st aircraft off the assembly line, deliveries of this version commencing spring 1969. Total ordered by beginning of 1975 in excess of 430 when production was continuing at 3–4 per month.

Notes: Series 100 and 200 Twin Otters feature a shorter nose and have 579 eshp PT6A-20s, and the Twin Otter is available as a floatplane. The Series 300S introduced in 1973 features upper wing spoilers, high-capacity brakes, an anti-skid braking system and other improvements.

DHC-6 TWIN OTTER SERIES 300

Dimensions: Span, 65 ft 0 in (19,81 m); length, 51 ft 9 in (15,77 m); height, 18 ft 7 in (5,66 m); wing area, 420 sq ft (39,02 m²).

DE HAVILLAND CANADA DHC-7 DASH-7

Country of Origin: Canada.
Type: STOL short-haul commercial transport.
Power Plant: Four 1,120 shp UACL PT6A-50 turboprops.
Performance: (Estimated) Max. cruise, 274 mph (441 km/h) at 7,500 ft (2 286 m); long-range cruise, 230 mph (370 km/h) at 20,000 ft (6 096 m); range with max. payload (11,060 lb/5 017 kg), 733 mls (1 180 km), with max. fuel, 2,003 mls (3 223 km).
Weights: Operational empty, 24,440 lb (11 130 kg); max. take-off, 41,000 lb (18 597 kg).
Accommodation: Flight crew of two and basic accommodation for 48 passengers with optional arrangement for 54 passengers.
Status: First of two pre-production aircraft was scheduled to commence its flight test programme in February 1975 with current planning calling for the first production deliveries to commence in the first quarter of 1977. Long-lead items for initial batch of 25 aircraft ordered late 1974, production approval having been given in late November of that year when orders had been received for a total of seven aircraft.
Notes: The result of a world-wide market survey of short-haul transport requirements, the DHC-7 STOL (short take-off and landing) airliner is being jointly funded by de Havilland Canada, United Aircraft (manufacturers of the engines) and the Canadian Government, and the US Boeing concern is expected to provide marketing support. The aircraft has been designed to operate with a full load of passengers from 2,000-ft (610-m) runways and will feature a quiet engine/propeller combination which will limit external noise during take-off and landing. The two pre-production examples of the DHC-7 are being built on production tooling and are fully representative of the production standard.

DE HAVILLAND CANADA DHC-7 DASH-7

Dimensions: Span, 93 ft 0 in (28,35 m); length, 80 ft 4 in (24,50 m); height, 26 ft 3 in (8,00 m); wing area, 860 sq ft (79,9 m²).

EMBRAER EMB-110 BANDEIRANTE

Country of Origin: Brazil.

Type: Light general-purpose and utility aircraft.

Power Plant: Two 680 shp UACL PT6A-27 turboprops.

Performance: Max. cruise, 282 mph (454 km/h) at 9,840 ft (3 000 m); max. range (with 30 min reserves), 1,273 mls (2 050 km); initial climb, 1,968 ft/min (10 m/sec); service ceiling (at 10,692 lb/4 850 kg), 27,950 ft (8 520 m).

Weights: Empty equipped, 7,054 lb (3 200 kg); max. take-off, 11,684 lb (5 300 kg).

Accommodation: Pilot and co-pilot side-by-side on flight deck with full dual controls. Standard cabin arrangement provides six individual seats on each side of central aisle. High-density arrangement for 16 passengers. Accommodation for four stretchers and two attendants.

Status: First of three prototypes flown October 26, 1968, with second and third following on October 19, 1969, and June 25, 1970, respectively. The first pre-series aircraft flew on August 15, 1972, and production tempo was scheduled to attain four per month by the beginning of 1975 when some 50 had been delivered against total orders for approximately 110, including 80 aircraft for *Fòrça Aérea Brasileira*.

Notes: Being manufactured by EMBRAER (Emprêsa Brasileira de Aeronáutica SA), the Bandeirante is intended to fulfil light transport, liaison, aeromedical and navigational tasks in the *Fòrça Aérea Brasileira*. The civil version of the Bandeirante has been ordered by Transbrasil, Taxi Aéreo and VASP. A pressurised development with 1,070 ehp PT6A-45s and accommodating 21 passengers will fly mid-1975 as the EMB-120.

EMBRAER EMB-110 BANDEIRANTE

Dimensions: Span, 50 ft 2¼ in (15,30 m); length, 46 ft 8¼ in (14,22 m); height, 15 ft 6 in (4,73 m); wing area, 312·13 sq ft (29,00 m²).

FAIRCHILD A-10A

Country of Origin: USA.
Type: Single-seat close-support aircraft.
Power Plant: Two 8,985 lb (4 075 kg) General Electric TF34-GE-100 turbofans.
Performance: Max. speed at 25,500 lb (11 567 kg), 461 mph (742 km/h) at sea level; max. design, 518 mph (833 km/h); mission radius (with 9,500 lb/4 309 kg useful pay-load and including 2 hrs loiter at 200 mph/322 km/h at 5,000 ft/1 525 m and 10 min combat at 345 mph/555 km/h at sea level), 300 mls (480 km) cruising at 357 mph (574 km/h) at 25,000 ft (7 620 m); ferry range, 2,648 mls (4 260 km).
Weights: Empty, 18,787 lb (8 522 kg); max. take-off, 45,202 lb (20 504 kg).
Armament: One 30-mm General Electric GAU-8/A cannon and up to 18,500 lb (8 392 kg) of ordnance on 11 external pylons. Typical possible loads include 24 Mk. 82 500-lb (227-kg) bombs, 16 M-117 750-lb (340-kg) bombs, four Mk. 84 2,000-lb (907-kg) bombs, 20 Rockeye 11 cluster bombs, or nine AGM-65 Maverick missiles.
Status: First of two prototypes flown May 10, 1972, fol-lowed by second on July 21, 1972. First of a batch of six research and development aircraft was scheduled to fly February 1975, and funding has been voted for an initial batch of 25 production aircraft.
Notes: Designed to meet the USAF's A-X close-support aircraft requirement, the A-10A participated in a fly-off con-test with the Northrop A-9A (see 1972 edition). The A-10A was announced winning contender on January 18, 1973.

FAIRCHILD A-10A

Dimensions: Span, 55 ft 0 in (16,76 m); length, 52 ft 7 in (16,03 m); height, 14 ft 5½ in (4,41 m); wing area, 488 sq ft (45,13 m²).

FAIRCHILD-SWEARINGEN METRO II

Country of Origin: USA.
Type: Commuter and third-level airliner.
Power Plant: Two 940 shp Garrett AiResearch TPE-331-3UW-303G turboprops.
Performance: Max. cruise, 294 mph (473 km/h) at 10,000 ft (3 050 m); range cruise, 279 mph (449 km/h) at 20,000 ft (6 100 m); range (with 45 min reserves), 215 mls (346 km) with 19 passengers, 685 mls (1 102 km) with 15 passengers; initial climb, 2,400 ft/min (12,2 m/sec); service ceiling (at 12,000 lb/5 443 kg), 27,000 ft (8 230 m).
Weights: Max. take-off, 12,500 lb (5 670 kg).
Accommodation: Flight crew of two and standard accommodation for max. of 21 passengers seated two abreast on each side of central aisle. Moveable bulkhead permitting mix of passengers and cargo.
Status: Prototype of corporate executive equivalent of Metro (Merlin IV) flown on August 26, 1969. Fourteen Metros delivered by beginning of 1975, with Metro II scheduled for delivery in spring of that year. Total production (Merlin IIIA and IVA, and Metro II) for 1975 expected to be 36 aircraft.
Notes: The Metro II is a commuter and third-level airliner version of the Merlin IVA which is, in turn, a stretched version of the Merlin IIIA. The Metro II and Merlin IVA differ externally from the original Metro and Merlin IV (see 1971 edition) primarily in having rectangular rather than circular cabin windows. The Merlin IVA can attain higher speeds than the Metro II primarily as a result of a reduced bleed air requirement.

FAIRCHILD-SWEARINGEN METRO II

Dimensions: Span, 46 ft 3 in (14,10 m); length, 59 ft 4⅘ in (18,10 m); height, 16 ft 9⅘ in (5,10 m); wing area, 277·5 sq ft (25,78 m²).

FFA AS 202/18A BRAVO

Country of Origin: Switzerland.
Type: Light training and touring aircraft.
Power Plant: One 180 hp Avco Lycoming IO-360-B1B four-cylinder horizontally-opposed engine.
Performance: Max. cruise, 140 mph (225 km/h) at 8,040 ft (2 450 m); endurance, 3 hr 40 min; initial climb, 935 ft/min (4,75 m/sec); service ceiling, 18,045 ft (5 500 m).
Weights: Empty equipped, 1,510 lb (685 kg); max. take-off, 2,295 lb (1 041 kg).
Accommodation: Two persons side-by-side with dual controls and optional aft seat for third person.
Status: Developed jointly by FFA (Flug- & Fahrzeugwerke) in Switzerland and SIAI-Marchetti in Italy, the first Swiss-built prototype of the Bravo was flown on March 7, 1969, followed by an Italian-assembled prototype on May 7 of the same year. The FFA has since been responsible for the production and marketing of this aircraft, completing a pre-production batch of 10 AS 202/15 Bravos and initiating, in 1974, an initial production batch of 20 aircraft which includes both AS 202/15 and AS 202/18A versions.
Notes: A fully-aerobatic aircraft aimed primarily at the civil and military basic training market, the Bravo is currently offered in two versions, the AS 202/15 with the 150 hp Lycoming O-320-E2A engine and the AS 202/18A described above. A version with a 115 hp Lycoming O-235-C2A engine, the AS 202/10, has been proposed.

FFA AS 202/18A BRAVO

Dimensions: Span, 31 ft 11¾ in (99,75 m); length, 24 ft 7¼ in (7,50 m); height, 9 ft 2¾ in (2,81 m); wing area, 149 sq ft (13,86 m²).

FOKKER F.27 FRIENDSHIP SRS. 500

Country of Origin: Netherlands.
Type: Short- to medium-range commercial transport.
Power Plant: Two 2,250 eshp Rolls-Royce Dart 532-7 turboprops.
Performance: Max. cruise, 322 mph (518 km/h) at 20,000 ft (6 095 m); normal cruise at 38,000 lb (17 237 kg), 298 mph (480 km/h) at 20,000 ft (6 095 m); range with max. payload, 667 mls (1 075 km), with max. fuel and 9,680-lb (4 390-kg) payload, 1,099 mls (1 805 km); initial climb at max. take-off weight, 1,200 ft/min (6,1 m/sec); service ceiling at 38,000 lb (17 237 kg), 29,500 ft (9 000 m).
Weights: Empty, 24,886 lb (11 288 kg); operational empty, 25,951 lb (11 771 kg); max. take-off, 45,000 lb (20 411 kg).
Accommodation: Basic flight crew of two or three and standard seating for 52 passengers. Alternative arrangements for up to 56 passengers.
Status: First Srs. 500 flown November 15, 1967. Production currently standardising on Srs. 500 and 600. Orders for the Friendship (including 205 licence-built in the USA by Fairchild) totalled 623 by beginning of 1975 when production rate was two per month.
Notes: By comparison with basic Srs. 200 (see 1968 edition), the Srs. 500 has a 4 ft 11 in (1,5 m) fuselage stretch. The Srs. 400 "Combiplane" (see 1966 edition) and the equivalent military Srs. 400M (illustrated above) are convertible cargo or combined cargo-passenger versions of the Srs. 200, and the current Srs. 600 is similar to the Srs. 400 but lacks the reinforced and watertight cargo floor.

FOKKER F.27 FRIENDSHIP SRS. 500

Dimensions: Span, 95 ft $1\frac{3}{4}$ in (29,00 m); length, 82 ft $2\frac{1}{2}$ in (25,06 m); height, 28 ft $7\frac{1}{4}$ in (8,71 m); wing area, 753·47 sq ft (70 m²).

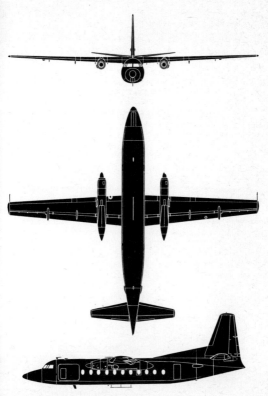

FOKKER F.28 FELLOWSHIP MK. 6000

Country of Origin: Netherlands.
Type: Short-range commercial transport.
Power Plant: Two 9,675 lb (4 390 kg) Rolls-Royce Spey Mk. 555-1H turbofans.
Performance: (At 70,000 lb/31 752 kg) 528 mph (849 km/h) at 21,000 ft (6 400 m); long-range cruise, 420 mph (676 km/h) at 30,000 ft (9 150 m); range with max. payload, 1,025 mls (1 650 km), with max. fuel (and 27 passengers), 1,197 mls (1 927 km).
Weights: Operating empty, 37,760 lb (17 127 kg); max. take-off, 70,000 lb (31 752 kg).
Accommodation: Flight crew of two with single-class accommodation for up to 79 passengers in five-abreast seating.
Status: The prototype Fellowship Mk. 6000 (the fuselage of the prototype Mk. 2000 and the modified wings of the second Mk. 1000 prototype) flew September 27, 1973, and production deliveries are scheduled for early 1975. Some 90 F.28s had been ordered by the beginning of 1975 with production tempo currently building up from 1·7 to two per month by early 1976.
Notes: The Fellowship Mk. 6000 is a derivative of the stretched-fuselage Mk. 2000, offering improved field performance and payload/range capabilities. Wing span is increased by 4 ft 11½ in (1,50 m), three-section leading-edge slats are added to each wing, and an uprated, quieter version of the Spey engine is employed. Similar changes to the basic (shorter-fuselage) Fellowship Mk. 1000 will result in the Fellowship Mk. 5000. All four variants of the Fellowship are to be offered in parallel.

FOKKER F.28 FELLOWSHIP MK. 6000

Dimensions: Span, 82 ft 3¾ in (25,09 m); length, 97 ft 1¼ in (29,61 m); height, 27 ft 9½ in (8,47 m); wing area, 850 sq ft (78,97 m²).

GAF NOMAD

Country of Origin: Australia.

Type: STOL utility transport.

Power Plant: Two 400 eshp Allison 250-B17 turboprops.

Performance: (Nomad 24 at 8,000 lb/3 629 kg) Max. cruise, 199 mph (320 km/h) at sea level, 202 mph (325 km/h) at 5,000 ft (1 524 m); long-range cruise, 161 mph (259 km/h) at 10,000 ft (3 048 m); max. range at 199 mph (320 km/h) at 10,000 ft (3 048 m) with 45 min reserves, 944 mls (1 518 km), with 1,600-lb (726-kg) payload, 725 mls (1 167 km) at max. cruise at sea level; initial climb, 1,500 ft/min (7,62 m/sec).

Weights: (Nomad 24) Basic empty, 4,330 lb (1 964 kg); max. take-off, 8,000 lb (3 629 kg).

Accommodation: Flight crew of either one or two, and up to 15 passengers in individual seats.

Status: First and second prototypes of Nomad 22 flown July 23, 1971, and December 5, 1971, respectively. Initial production batch of 20 Nomad 22s with follow-on batch of 50 Nomad 22s and 24s authorised by beginning of 1975 when some 50 aircraft were on order.

Notes: Nomad 24 (general arrangement drawing) differs from Nomad 22 (second prototype of which is illustrated above) in having plugs in the fuselage fore and aft of the wing. Initial production batch confined to short-fuselage Nomad 22, and GAF (Government Aircraft Factories) to deliver 11 of first batch of 20 to Australian Army Aviation.

GAF NOMAD

Dimensions: Span, 54 ft 0 in (16,46 m); length, 47 ft 0 in (14,30 m(; height, 18 ft 0 in (5,48 m); wing area, 320 sq ft (29,7 m²).

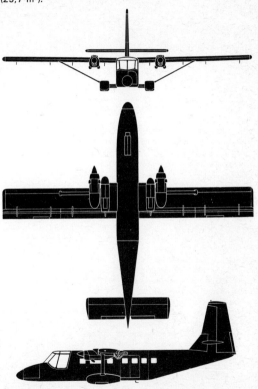

GATES LEARJET 35

Country of Origin: USA.
Type: Light business executive transport.
Power Plant: Two 3,500 lb (1 588 kg) Garrett AiResearch TFE 731-2 turbofans.
Performance: Max. speed, 548 mph (882 km/h); max. range, 3,028 mls (4 875 km); range with max. payload (1,914 lb/868 kg), 2,572 mls (4 140 km); initial climb, 5,150 ft/min (26 m/sec); service ceiling, 42,500 ft (12 950 m).
Weights: Operational empty, 9,142 lb (4 146 kg); max. take-off, 17,000 lb (7 711 kg).
Accommodation: Two pilots or pilot and passenger on flight deck and up to seven passengers in main cabin.
Status: Prototype Learjet 35 flown on August 22, 1973, with first customer deliveries initiated late 1974. Production of all versions running at eight per month at beginning of 1975 with some 500 delivered.
Notes: The latest additions to the Learjet range, the Models 35 and 36, feature marginally longer fuselages and longer-span wings by comparison with the Model 25 which was previously the largest Learjet, and turbofans supplant the General Electric CJ610 turbojets employed by earlier models such as the Model 24D (see 1971 edition). The Models 35 and 36 are dimensionally similar, the latter (illustrated above) accommodating up to six passengers and offering greater range (3,620 mls/5 826 km). Production of the Models 24D, 25B and 25C is continuing the 24D having a 43 ft 3 in (13,18 m) fuselage and the 25B and 25C being 4 ft 2 in (1,27 m) longer, the last-mentioned model possessing increased fuel capacity.

GATES LEARJET 35

Dimensions: Span, 39 ft 8 in (12,09 m); length, 48 ft 8 in (14,83 m); height, 12 ft 3 in (3,73 m); wing area, 253·3 sq ft (23,5 m²).

GENERAL DYNAMICS YF-16

Country of Origin: USA.

Type: Single-seat air superiority fighter.

Power Plant: One 23,500 lb (10 650 kg) reheat Pratt & Whitney F100-PW-100 turbofan.

Performance: Estimated max. speed, 835 mph (1 344 km/h) at 1,000 ft (305 m) or Mach 1·1, 1,450 mph (2 333 km/h) above 36,000 ft (10 970 m) or Mach 2·2; approx. combat radius on internal fuel (air superiority role), 550+ mls (885+ km); ferry range, 2,500+ mls (4 020+ km); absolute ceiling, 60,000+ ft (18 290+ m).

Weights: Normal take-off (air superiority role), 17,500 lb (7 938 kg); max. take-off (close support role), 27,000 lb (12 250 kg).

Armament: One 20-mm M-61A Vulcan rotary cannon and two AIM-9E or -9J Sidewinder AAMs for air superiority role. Up to 8,000 lb (3 992 kg) of external ordnance for the close support role on seven external hardpoints.

Status: First prototype flown on January 20, 1974, with second prototype following on May 9, 1974.

Notes: Featuring such advanced features as a fly-by-wire control system with no mechanical linkage between controls and control surfaces and blended wing/body design, the YF-16 (Model 401) was, like the Northrop YF-17 (see pages 150–151) originally developed for the study of lightweight fighter technology but, during the course of 1974, participated in a competitive fly-off with its Northrop contemporary for selection as the basis of the USAF's ACF (Air Combat Fighter) which is scheduled to be delivered to the service from 1978.

GENERAL DYNAMICS YF-16

Dimensions: Span, 30 ft 0 in (9,14 m); length (excluding nose probe), 46 ft 6 in (14,17 m); height, 16 ft 3 in (4,95 m).

GRUMMAN A-6 INTRUDER

Country of Origin: USA.

Type: Two-seat shipboard low-level strike aircraft.

Power Plant: Two 9,300 lb (4 218 kg) Pratt & Whitney J52-P-8A turbojets.

Performance: Max. speed at 36,655 lb (16 626 kg) in clean condition, 685 mph (1 102 km/h) or Mach 0·9 at sea level, 625 mph (1 006 km/h) or Mach 0·94 at 36,000 ft (10 970 m); average cruise, 480 mph (772 km/h) at 32,750–43,800 ft (9 980–13 350 m); range with max. internal fuel and four Bullpup ASMs, 1,920 mls (3 090 km), with single store and four 250 Imp gal (1 136 l) external tanks, 3,040 mls (4 890 km).

Weights: Empty, 25,684 lb (11 650 kg); loaded (clean), 37,116 lb (16 836 kg); max. overload take-off, 60,280 lb (27 343 kg).

Armament: Max. external ordnance load of 15,000 lb (6 804 kg) distributed between five 3,600-lb (1 633-kg) stores stations.

Status: First of eight test and development aircraft flown April 19, 1960 and first delivery to US Navy (A-6A) on February 7, 1963.

Notes: Specification relates to basic A-6A (see 1970 edition), drawing depicts A-6B which differs in having equipment for AGM-78A Standard ARM (Anti-Radiation Missile), and the photograph above illustrates the A-6E with TRAM (Target Recognition Attack Multisensor) in under-nose turreted housing, this providing lower hemispheric coverage for laser-guided weapon delivery. The A-6E has more advanced avionics and flew in prototype form on February 27, 1970, first deliveries to the US Navy following in 1971, with 72 funded by 1974 from planned total procurement of 192. Additional 192 A-6Es resulting from retrofit of A-6As.

GRUMMAN A-6 INTRUDER

Dimensions: Span, 53 ft 0 in (16,15 m); length, 54 ft 7 in (16,64 m); height, 15 ft 7 in (4,75 m); wing area, 529 sq ft (49,15 m²).

GRUMMAN F-14A TOMCAT

Country of Origin: USA.

Type: Two-seat shipboard multi-purpose fighter.

Power Plant: Two 20,900 lb (9 480 kg) reheat Pratt & Whitney TF30-P-412 turbofans.

Performance: Design max. speed (clean), 1,545 mph (2 486 km/h) at 40,000 ft (12 190 m) or Mach 2·34; max. speed (internal fuel and four AIM-7 missiles at 55,000 lb/24 948 kg), 910 mph (1 470 km/h) at sea level or Mach 1·2; tactical radius (internal fuel and four AIM-7 missiles plus allowance for 2 min combat at 10,000 ft/3 050 m), approx. 450 mls (725 km); time to 60,000 ft (18 290 m) at 55,000 lb (24 948 kg), 2·1 min.

Weights: Empty equipped, 40,070 lb (18 176 kg); normal take-off (internal fuel and four AIM-7 AAMs), 55,000 lb (24 948 kg); max. take-off (ground attack/interdiction), 68,567 lb (31 101 kg).

Armament: One 20-mm M-61A1 rotary cannon and (intercept mission) six AIM-7E/F Sparrow and four AIM-9G/H Sidewinder AAMs or six AIM-54A and two AIM-9G/H AAMs.

Status: First of 12 research and development aircraft flown December 21, 1970. Total of 234 ordered by 1975 (with 121 delivered) against procurement for US Navy and USMC of 334. Eighty ordered for Iran with deliveries commencing early 1976. Current production rate of 6–7 per month.

Notes: First of two F-14B prototypes powered by 28,096 lb (12 745 kg) reheat Pratt & Whitney F401-PW-400 turbofans flown on September 12, 1973. No production plans for this version exist.

GRUMMAN F-14A TOMCAT

Dimensions: Span (max.), 64 ft $1\frac{1}{2}$ in (19,55 m), (min.), 37 ft 7 in (11,45 m), (overswept on deck), 33 ft $3\frac{1}{2}$ in (10,15 m); length, 61 ft $11\frac{7}{8}$ in (18,90 m); height, 16 ft 0 in (4,88 m); wing area, 565 sq ft (52,5 m²).

GRUMMAN AMERICAN TIGER

Country of Origin: USA.

Type: Light cabin monoplane.

Power Plant: One 180 hp Avco Lycoming O-360-A1D four-cylinder horizontally-opposed engine.

Performance: Max. speed, 170 mph (273 km/h) at sea level; cruise (75% power), 160 mph (257 km/h) at 9,000 ft (2 743 m); cruising range (at 75% power), 650 mls (1 046 km); initial climb, 850 ft/min (4,31 m/sec).

Weights: Empty equipped, 1,285 lb (583 kg); max. take-off, 2,400 lb (1 089 kg).

Accommodation: Pilot and three passengers in paired separate seats beneath aft-sliding canopy.

Status: Tiger introduced autumn 1974 with first customer deliveries late 1974. Production deliveries of Grumman American light cabin monoplanes (i.e., AA-1B Trainer, AA-5 Traveller and Tiger) averaged 40 per month during 1974 and are expected to increase to 50 per month during the course of 1975.

Notes: The Tiger is essentially a re-engined Traveller (see 1974 edition) with a lengthened nose, revised wheel spats, extended cabin glazing and revised tail surfaces. The AA-5 Traveller is powered by a 150 hp Avco Lycoming O-320-E2G engine and is, in turn, an enlarged and more powerful version of the AA-1B Trainer side-by-side two-seater (see 1972 edition).

GRUMMAN AMERICAN TIGER

Dimensions: Span, 31 ft 6 in (9,60 m); length, 22 ft 0 in (6,70 m); height, 8 ft 2½ in (2,50 m); wing area, 140 sq ft (13,01 m²).

HAWKER SIDDELEY 125 SERIES 600

Country of Origin: United Kingdom.
Type: Light business executive transport.
Power Plant: Two 3,750 lb (1 700 kg) Rolls-Royce Viper 601 turbojets.
Performance: Max. cruise, 518 mph (834 km/h) at 27,000 ft (8 230 m); long-range cruise, 503 mph (810 km/h) at 40,000 ft (12 192 m); range (max. fuel and 1,600-lb/725-kg payload plus 45 min reserves), 1,876 mls (3 020 km), (with 2,359-lb/1 070-kg payload), 1,785 mls (2 872 km).
Weights: Empty equipped, 12,148 lb (5 510 kg); max. take-off, 25,000 lb (11 340 kg).
Accommodation: Normal flight crew of two and basic arrangement for eight passengers with alternative arrangements available for up to 14 passengers.
Status: Two Series 600 development aircraft flown on January 21, 1971, and November 25, 1971. Production deliveries began early 1973.
Notes: The Series 600 is the current production version of the basic HS.125, this being essentially a higher-powered, stretched version of the Series 400 which it replaces. An additional 2-ft (0,62-m) section has been inserted in the fuselage ahead of the wing leading edge, this allowing two more seats to be offered in the cabin; a nose radome of improved profile has been adopted; the upper fuselage contours have been revised, and taller vertical tail surfaces have been introduced. Aircraft completed to US standards are being marketed in the USA by Beech as the BH.125-600A and sales of Series 600 aircraft totalled some 70 by the beginning of 1975. Series 600 preceded by 101 Series 400 aircraft and 148 examples of earlier models plus two prototypes and 20 of a navigational training version (Dominie).

HAWKER SIDDELEY 125 SERIES 600

Dimensions: Span, 47 ft 0 in (14,32 m); length, 50 ft 5¾ in (15,37 m); height, 17 ft 3 in (5,26 m); wing area, 353 sq ft (32,8 m²).

HAWKER SIDDELEY 748 SERIES 2A

Country of Origin: United Kingdom.

Type: Short- to medium-range commercial transport.

Power Plant: Two 2,280 ehp Rolls-Royce Dart R.Da.7 Mk. 532-2L turboprops.

Performance: Max. speed at 40,000 lb (18 145 kg), 312 mph (502 km/h) at 16,000 ft (4 875 m); max. cruise, 287 mph (462 km/h) at 15,000 ft (4 570 m); econ. cruise, 267 mph (430 km/h) at 20,000 ft (6 095 m); range cruise, 259 mph (418 km/h) at 25,000 ft (7 620 m); range with max. fuel and reserves for 45 min hold and 230-mile (370-km) diversion, 1,862 mls (2 996 km), with max. payload and same reserves, 690 mls (1 110 km).

Weights: Basic operational, 25,361 lb (11 504 kg); max. take-off, 44,495 lb (20 182 kg).

Accommodation: Normal flight crew of two and standard cabin arrangement for 40 passengers on paired seats.

Status: First prototype flown June 24, 1960, and first production model (Series 1) on August 30, 1961. Series 1 superseded by Series 2 in 1962, this being in turn superseded by current Series 2A from mid-1967. Total of 299 ordered by beginning of 1975.

Notes: Assembled under licence in India by HAL for Indian Airlines (24) and Indian Air Force (four Series 1 and 41 Series 2), with 69th and last completed early 1975 when a decision concerning Indian assembly of a further batch was awaited. The Series 2C flown on December 31, 1971, is similar to the Series 2A apart from the addition of a large rear freight door and is illustrated above, purchasers of the last-mentioned version including the Belgian Air Force.

HAWKER SIDDELEY 748 SERIES 2A

Dimensions: Span, 98 ft 6 in (30,02 m); length, 67 ft 0 in (20,42 m); height, 24 ft 10 in (7,57 m); wing area, 810·75 sq ft (75,35 m²).

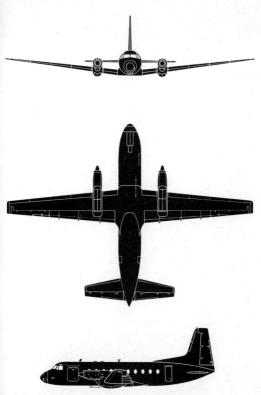

HAWKER SIDDELEY BUCCANEER
S. MK. 2B

Country of Origin: United Kingdom.
Type: Two-seat strike and reconnaissance aircraft.
Power Plant: Two 11,100 lb (5 035 kg) Rolls-Royce RB.
168-1A Spey Mk. 101 turbofans.
Performance: (Estimated) Max. speed, 645 mph (1 040
km/h) or Mach 0·85 at 250 ft (75 m), 620 mph (998 km/h)
or Mach 0·92 at 30,000 ft (9 145 m); typical low-level
cruise, 570 mph (917 km/h) or Mach 0·75 at 3,000 ft
(915 m); tactical radius for hi-lo-lo-hi mission with standard
fuel, 500–600 mls (805–965 km).
Weights: Max. take-off, 59,000 lb (26 762 kg).
Armament: Max. ordnance load of 16,000 lb (7 257 kg),
including four 500-lb (227-kg), 540-lb (245-kg), or 1,000-lb
(453,5-kg) bombs internally, and up to three 1,000-lb
(453,5-kg) or six 500-lb (227-kg) bombs on each of four
wing stations.
Status: First S. Mk. 2B for RAF flown January 8, 1970, with
deliveries of 42 built to this standard continuing into 1975.
Proportion of 84 S. Mk. 2s built for Royal Navy being modified for RAF use as S. Mk. 2As, and most of these ultimately
to be converted to S. Mk. 2Bs.
Notes: The S. Mk. 2A embodies avionic, system and equipment modifications for RAF service. Wing and weapon-pylon
changes to provide Martel missile capability characterise the
S. Mk. 2B which introduces 425 Imp gal (1 932 l) fuel tank
on rotating bomb door (seen on accompanying drawing) and
undercarriage changes to accommodate new gross weight of
59,000 lb (26 762 kg). The Navy versions are S. Mk. 2C and
S. Mk. 2D without and with Martel respectively.

HAWKER SIDDELEY BUCCANEER S. MK. 2B

Dimensions: Span, 44 ft 0 in (13,41 m); length, 63 ft 5 in (19,33 m); height, 16 ft 3 in (4,95 m); wing area, 514·7 sq ft (47,82 m²).

HAWKER SIDDELEY HARRIER G.R. MK. 3

Country of Origin: United Kingdom.
Type: Single-seat V/STOL strike and reconnaissance fighter.
Power Plant: One 21,500 lb (9 760 kg) Rolls-Royce Bristol Pegasus 103 vectored-thrust turbofan.
Performance: Max. speed, 720 mph (1 160 km/h) or Mach 0·95 at 1,000 ft (305 m), with typical external ordnance load, 640–660 mph (1 030–1 060 km) or Mach 0·85–0·87 at 1,000 ft (305 m); cruise, 560 mph (900 km/h) or Mach 0·8 at 20,000 ft (6 096 m); tactical radius for hi-lo-hi mission, 260 mls (418 km), with two 100 Imp gal (455 l) external tanks, 400 mls (644 km); ferry range with four 330 Imp gal (1 500 l) external tanks, 2,070 mls (3 330 km).
Weights: Empty, 12,400 lb (5 624 kg); max. take-off (VTO), 18,000 lb (8 165 kg); max. take-off (STO), 23,000+ lb (10 433+ kg); approx. max. take-off, 26,000 lb (11 793 kg).
Armament: Provision for two 30-mm Aden cannon with 130 rpg and up to 5,000 lb (2 268 kg) of ordnance on five external hardpoints.
Status: First of six pre-production aircraft flown August 31, 1966, with first of 77 G.R. Mk. 1s for RAF following December 28, 1967. Production of G.R. Mk. 1s and 13 T. Mk. 2s (see 1969 edition) for RAF completed. Production of 102 Mk. 50s (equivalent to G.R. Mk. 3) and eight two-seaters (equivalent to T. Mk. 4) for US Marine Corps continuing through 1975, first having been delivered January 26, 1971. Follow-on order for 15 G.R. Mk. 3s placed March 1973.
Notes: RAF Harrier G.R. Mk. 1s and T. Mk. 2s converted to G. R. Mk. 1As and T. Mk. 2As by installation of 20,000 lb (9 100 kg) Pegasus 102. These are to be progressively modified as G.R. Mk. 3s and T. Mk. 4s by installation of Pegasus 103 similar to that installed in Mk. 50 (AV-8A) for USMC. The G.R. Mk. 3s are to be fitted with nose-mounted laser rangefinder, new nose shape being illustrated.

HAWKER SIDDELEY HARRIER G.R. MK. 3

Dimensions: Span, 25 ft 3 in (7,70 m); length, 45 ft 7¾ in (13,91 m); height, 11 ft 3 in (3,43 m); wing area, 201·1 sq ft (18,68 m²).

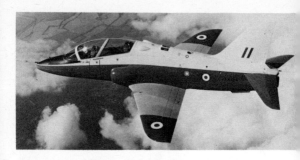

HAWKER SIDDELEY HAWK T.MK.1

Country of Origin: United Kingdom.

Type: Two-seat multi-purpose trainer and light tactical aircraft.

Power Plant: One 5,340 lb (2 422 kg) Rolls-Royce Turboméca RT.172-06-11 Adour 151 turbofan.

Performance: Max. speed, 617 mph (993 km/h) at sea level, 570 mph (917 km/h) at 30,000 ft (9 144 m); range cruise, 405 mph (652 km/h) at 30,000 ft (9 144 m); time to 40,000 ft (12 192 m), 10 min; service ceiling, 44,000 ft (13 410 m).

Weights: Empty, 7,450 lb (3 379 kg); normal take-off (trainer), 10,250 lb (4 649 kg), (weapons trainer), 12,000 lb (5 443 kg); max. take-off, 16,500 lb (7 484 kg).

Armament: (Weapon trainer) One strong point on fuselage centreline and two wing strong points and (ground attack) two additional wing strong points, all stressed for loads up to 1,000 lb (454 kg). Max. external load of 5,000 lb (2 268 kg).

Status: Single pre-production example flown on August 21, 1974, and first production example was expected to fly at the beginning of 1975. Total of 175 on order for RAF with 10 being scheduled for delivery to that service during 1976 and production then running at 3–4 per month until completion of order in 1980.

Notes: The Hawk is to be used by the RAF in the basic and advanced flying training and weapons training roles, and a single-seat ground attack version is being offered for export.

HAWKER SIDDELEY HAWK T.MK.1

Dimensions: Span, 30 ft 10 in (9,40 m); length (including probe), 39 ft 2½ in (11,96 m); height, 13 ft 5 in (4,10 m); wing area, 180 sq ft (16,70 m²).

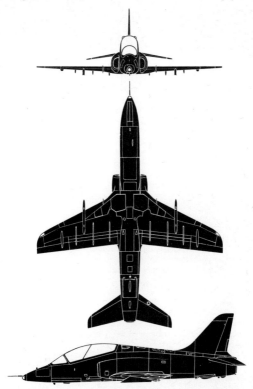

HAWKER SIDDELEY NIMROD M.R. MK. 1

Country of Origin: United Kingdom.
Type: Long-range maritime patrol aircraft.
Power Plant: Four 12,160 lb (5 515 kg) Rolls-Royce RB. 168-20 Spey Mk. 250 turbofans.
Performance: Max. speed, 575 mph (926 km/h); max. transit speed, 547 mph (880 km/h); econ. transit speed, 490 mph (787 km/h); typical ferry range, 5,180–5,755 mls (8 340–9 265 km); typical endurance, 12 hrs.
Weights: Max. take-off, 177,500 lb (80 510 kg); max. overload (eight new-build Mk. 1s), 192,000 lb (87 090 kg).
Armament: Ventral weapons bay accommodating full range of ASW weapons (homing torpedoes, mines, depth charges, etc) plus two underwing pylons on each side for total of four Aérospatiale AS.12 ASMs (or AS.11 training rounds).
Accommodation: Normal operating crew of 12 with two pilots and flight engineer on flight deck and nine navigators and sensor operators in tactical compartment.
Status: First of two Nimrod prototypes employing modified Comet 4C airframes flown May 23, 1967. First of initial batch of 38 production Nimrod M.R. Mk. 1s flown on June 28, 1968. Completion of this batch in August 1972 followed by delivery of three Nimrod R. Mk. 1s for special electronics reconnaissance, and eight more M.R. Mk. 1s on order with deliveries continuing through 1975.
Notes: Entire fleet to undergo refit programme as Nimrod M.R. Mk. 2s with updated avionics and communications fit and service entry from 1978. Changes will include new EMI radar, a new sonics system, a navigation system of improved accuracy, increased computer capacity and improved display system techniques.

HAWKER SIDDELEY NIMROD M.R. MK. 1

Dimensions: Span, 114 ft 10 in (35,00 m); length, 126 ft 9 in (38,63 m); height, 29 ft 8½ in (9,01 m); wing area, 2,121 sq ft (197,05 m²).

HAWKER SIDDELEY TRIDENT 2E

Country of Origin: United Kingdom.

Type: Medium-haul commercial transport.

Power Plant: Three 11,930 lb (5 411 kg) Rolls-Royce RB.163-25 Mk. 512-5W/50 turbofans.

Performance: Max. cruise, 596 mph (959 km/h) at 30,000 ft (9 144 m); long-range cruise, 504 mph (891 km/h) at 35,000 ft (10 668 m); range with max. payload (29 600 lb/ 13 426 kg), 3,155 mls (5 077 km), with max. fuel at long-range cruise, 3,558 mls (5 726 km).

Weights: Operational empty, 73,200 lb (33 203 kg); max. take-off, 143,500 lb (65,090 kg).

Accommodation: Flight crew of three and alternative arrangements for 12 first-class and 79 tourist-class passengers or (BEA) 97 tourist-class passengers in six-abreast seating.

Status: Principal current production model of the Trident at the beginning of 1974 was the 2E which was being built against orders for 33 (plus two Super 3Bs) for the People's Republic of China. The first Trident 2E flew on July 27, 1967, 15 subsequently being delivered to British Airways (BEA) and two to Cyprus Airways.

Notes: The Trident 2E differs from the earlier Trident 1C and 1E (see 1966 edition) in having uprated engines, increased weights, Kücheman wingtips and increased span, fuel and weights. Twenty-four Trident 1Cs and 15 1Es were built. The Trident 3B (see 1973 edition) is a high-capacity short-haul development of the Trident 1E with a stretched fuselage and similar power plants and wing modifications to those of the 2E. Twenty-six Trident 3Bs were built for British Airways (BEA) with the last being delivered in April 1973. The Trident Super 3B offers accommodation for 152 passengers and carries additional fuel in the wing centre section.

HAWKER SIDDELEY TRIDENT 2E

Dimensions: Span, 98 ft 0 in (29,87 m); length, 114 ft 9 in (34,97 m); height, 27 ft 0 in (8,23 m); wing area, 1,462 sq ft (135,82 m²).

ICA-BRASOV IAR-823

Country of Origin: Romania.
Type: Light cabin monoplane.
Power Plant: One 290 hp Avco Lycoming IO-540-G1D5 six-cylinder horizontally-opposed engine.
Performance: Max. speed, 186 mph (300 km/h) at sea level; cruise at 75% power, 175 mph (280 km/h) at 5,750 ft (1 750 m); econ. cruise (60% power), 168 mph (270 km/h) at 10,000 ft (3 050 m); max. range, 820 mls (1 300 km); initial climb, 1,378 ft/min (7,0 m/sec); service ceiling, 19,025 ft (7,0 m/sec).
Weights: Empty, 1,940 lb (880 kg); max. take-off, 3,307 lb (1 500 kg).
Accommodation: Pilot and three passengers seated in pairs or (basic training version) side-by-side seating for instructor and pupil with full dual controls.
Status: First of two prototypes flown during July 1973, with first production deliveries scheduled to commence 1976.
Notes: The IAR-823 is to be offered both as a four-seat tourer and as a two-seat basic and weapons trainer. For the weapons training role it is to be equipped with two under-wing pylons for gun or rocket pods or practice bombs. Alternatively, one 15·4 Imp. gal (70 l) drop tank may be carried beneath each wing. At a weight of 2,618 lb (1 187 kg) the IAR-823 is aerobatic.

ICA-BRASOV IAR-823

Dimensions: Span, 32 ft 9¾ in (10,00 m); length, 27 ft 0¼ in (8,24 m); height, 8 ft 3¼ in (2,52 m); wing area, 161·5 sq ft (15,00 m²).

ILYUSHIN IL-38 (MAY)

Country of Origin: USSR.

Type: Long-range maritime patrol aircraft.

Power Plant: Four 4,250 ehp Ivchenko AI-20M turboprops.

Performance: (Estimated) Max. continuous cruise, 400 mph (645 km/h) at 15,000 ft (4 570 m); normal cruise, 370 mph (595 km/h) at 26,250 ft (8 000 m); patrol speed, 250 mph (400 km/h) at 2,000 ft (610 m); max. range, 4,500 mls (7 240 km); loiter endurance, 12 hrs at 2,000 ft (610 m).

Weights: (Estimated) Empty equipped, 80,000 lb (36 287 kg); max. take-off, 140,000 lb (63 500 kg).

Armament: Internal weapons bay for depth bombs, homing torpedoes, etc. Wing hardpoints for external ordnance loads.

Accommodation: Normal flight crew believed to consist of 12 members, of which half are housed by tactical compartment, operating sensors and co-ordinating data flow to surface vessels and other aircraft.

Status: The Il-38 reportedly flew in prototype form during 1967–68, entering service with the Soviet naval air arm early in 1970.

Notes: The Il-38 has been evolved from the Il-18 commercial transport in a similar fashion to the development of the Lockheed P-3 Orion from the Electra transport. Apart from some strengthening, the wings, tail assembly and undercarriage are similar to those of the Il-18. By comparison, the wing is positioned further forward on the fuselage for CG reasons. The Il-38 has been observed operating in the Mediterranean as well as over the seas surrounding the Soviet Union.

ILYUSHIN IL-38 (MAY)

Dimensions: Span, 122 ft 9 in (37,40 m); length, 131 ft 0 in (39,92 m); height, 33 ft 4 in (10,17 m); wing area, 1,507 sq ft (140,0 m²).

ILYUSHIN IL-76 (CANDID)

Country of Origin: USSR.
Type: Heavy commercial and military freighter.
Power Plant: Four 26,455 lb (12 000 kg) Soloviev D-30-KP turbofans.
Performance: Max. cruise, 528 mph (850 km/h) at 42,650 ft (13 000 m); range with max. payload (88,185 lb/40 000 kg), 3,107 mls (5 000 km).
Weights: Max. take-off, 346,122 lb (157 000 kg).
Accommodation: Normal flight crew of three—four on flight deck and in glazed nose, and pressurised hold for freight.
Status: First of four prototypes flown on March 25, 1971, with production deliveries to commence in 1974–5. Approximately 100 to be delivered to Aeroflot with initial service scheduled for 1975.
Notes: Apparently evolved primarily to meet a military requirement, the Il-76 is generally similar in concept to the Lockheed C-141A StarLifter, but is slightly larger, more powerful and heavier. It employs a mechanised cargo-handling system, a high-flotation undercarriage, the main members of which comprise four individual units each of four parallel-mounted wheels, and extensive high-lift devices to achieve short-field performance. According to an official Soviet statement, the Il-76 is intended to operate from short unprepared strips in Siberia and other undeveloped areas of the Soviet Union during the period of the current five-year programme (1971–75). Clam-shell thrust reversers are fitted to all four power plants.

112

ILYUSHIN IL-76 (CANDID)

Dimensions: Span, 165 ft 8⅓ in (50,50 m); length, 152 ft 10¼ in (46,59 m); height, 48 ft 5⅛ in (14,76 m).

KAWASAKI C-1A

Country of Origin: Japan.

Type: Medium-range military transport.

Power Plant: Two 14,500 lb (6 575 kg) Pratt & Whitney JT8D-9 turbofans.

Performance: Max. speed, 489 mph (787 km/h) at 25,000 ft (7 620 m); max. cruise, 426 mph (685 km/h) at 32,680 ft (10 670 m); range with max. fuel, 2,073 mls (3 335 km), with (normal) 17,637-lb (8 000-kg) payload, 806 mls (1 297 km); initial climb, 4,000 ft/min (20,3 m/sec); service ceiling, 39,370 ft (12 000 m).

Weights: Empty equipped, 53,131 lb (24 100 kg); max. take-off, 99,208 lb (45 000 kg).

Accommodation: Basic crew of five. Loads include 60 troops, 45 paratroops, or 36 casualty stretchers plus medical attendants. Cargo loads may include a 5,000-lb (2 268-kg) truck, a 105-mm howitzer, two 1,500-lb (680-kg) trucks, or three jeep-type vehicles.

Status: First of two flying prototypes flown on November 12, 1970, and second on January 16, 1971. First of two pre-production examples delivered 1973. Production deliveries initiated December 1974. A further 10 C-1As are expected to be delivered by March 1976 against total procurement of 26 aircraft during the current (1972–75) five-year defence programme. It is anticipated that an additional 12 C-1As will be purchased before 1978.

Notes: The C-1A is intended as a successor to the Curtiss C-46 transport, and a stretched version and an airborne early-warning derivative were being projected at the beginning of 1975.

KAWASAKI C-1A

Dimensions: Span, 100 ft $3\frac{3}{4}$ in (30,60 m); length, 95 ft $1\frac{3}{4}$ in (29,00 m); height, 32 ft $9\frac{3}{4}$ in (10,00 m); wing area, 1,297 sq ft (120,5 m²).

LET L 410 TURBOLET

Country of Origin: Czechoslovakia.
Type: Light utility transport, feederliner and (L 410AF) photographic survey aircraft.
Power Plant: Two 715 ehp UACL PT6A-27 turboprops.
Performance: Max. cruise, 235 mph (380 km/h) at 9,840 ft (3 000 m); econ. cruise, 205 mph (330 km/h) at 9,840 ft (3 000 m); range with max. fuel and 45 min reserves, 705 mls (1 140 km), with max. payload and same reserves, 115 mls (185 km); initial climb, 1,595 ft/min (8,1 m/sec); service ceiling, 25,490 ft (7 770 m).
Weights: Basic empty (freight version), 6,876 lb (3 100 kg); max. take-off, 11,905 lb (5 400 kg).
Accommodation: Flight crew of two and alternative arrangements for 12, 15, 19 or 20 passengers in rows of three with two seats to starboard and one to port. L 410AF photographic version has stations for camera operators in nose and main cabin. Business executive layout available with accommodation for eight passengers.
Status: First of four prototypes flown April 16, 1969. Pre-production series of six aircraft built during 1971 of which two entered service with Slov-Air in September of that year. First production deliveries (to Slov-Air) commenced in 1972, and photographic versions developed in 1973 with first deliveries (to Hungary) in 1974.
Notes: Development of variant with the indigenous M-601-B turboprop of 740 ehp continuing at beginning of 1975. The accompanying illustrations depict the photographic L 410AF.

LET L 410 TURBOLET

Dimensions: Span, 57 ft 3 in (17,50 m); length, 44 ft 7½ in (13,61 m); height, 18 ft 4 in (5,65 m); wing area, 349·83 sq ft (32,5 m²).

LOCKHEED L-1011-1 TRISTAR

Country of Origin: USA.

Type: Short- to medium-range commercial transport.

Power Plant: Three 42,000 lb (19 050 kg) Rolls-Royce RB.211-22B turbofans.

Performance: Max. cruise at max. take-off weight, 590 mph (950 km/h) at 35,000 ft (10 670 m); econ. cruise, 540 mph (870 km/h) at 35,000 ft (10 670 m); range with max. fuel and 40,000 lb (18 145 kg) payload, 4,467 mls (7 189 km); range with max. payload comprising 256 passengers and 5,000 lb (2 270 kg) cargo, 2,878 mls (4 629 km); initial climb 2,800 ft/min (14,2 m/sec).

Weights: Empty, 218,999 lb (99 336 kg); operational empty, 234,275 lb (106 265 kg); max. take-off, 430,000 lb (195 045 kg).

Accommodation: Basic flight crew of three–four. Typical passenger configuration provides 256 seats in a ratio of 20% first class and 80% coach class. An all-economy configuration provides for 345 passengers.

Status: First L-1011-1 flown November 16, 1970, with first deliveries (to Eastern) following in April 1972. By 1975 orders and "second buy" options totalled 209 aircraft.

Notes: The Model 193 (L-1011) TriStar is the first aircraft to employ the RB.211 engine, and at the beginning of 1975 an extended-range version of the basic design with RB.211-524 engines of 48,000 lb (21 772 kg) was under development as the L-1011-200, the first order for this version being placed by Saudia. The L-1011-100 (which supplants the L-1011-1) can have either RB.211-22B or -22F (43,500 lb/19 730 kg) engines.

LOCKHEED L-1011-1 TRISTAR

Dimensions: Span, 155 ft 4 in (47,34 m); length, 177 ft 8½ in (54,16 m); height, 55 ft 4 in (16,87 m); wing area, 3,755 sq ft (348,85 m²).

LOCKHEED C-130H HERCULES

Country of Origin: USA.

Type: Medium- to long-range military transport.

Power Plant: Four 4,050 eshp Allison T56-A-7A turboprops.

Performance: Max. speed, 384 mph (618 km/h); max. cruise, 368 mph (592 km/h); econ. cruise, 340 mph (547 km/h); range (with max. payload and 5% plus 30 min reserves), 2,450 mls (3 943 km); max. range, 4,770 mls (7 675 km); initial climb, 1,900 ft/min (9,65 m/sec).

Weights: Empty equipped, 72,892 lb (33 063 kg); max. normal take-off, 155,000 lb (70 310 kg); max. overload, 175,000 lb (79 380 kg).

Accommodation: Flight crew of four and max. of 92 fully-equipped troops, 64 paratroops, or 74 casualty stretchers and two medical attendants. As a cargo carrier up to six pre-loaded freight pallets may be carried.

Status: The C-130H is the principal current production version of the Hercules which, in progressively developed forms, has been in continuous production since 1952, and at the beginning of 1975, when more than 1,300 Hercules had been ordered, production rate was being raised to six per month.

Notes: The C-130H, which was in process of delivery to the USAF, Abu Dhabi, Brazil, Canada, Denmark, Greece, Malaysia, Nigeria, Saudi Arabia and Morocco, at the beginning of 1975, is basically a C-130E with more powerful engines, and the Hercules C Mk. 1 (C-130K) serving with the RAF differs in having some UK-supplied instruments, avionics and other items.

LOCKHEED C-130H HERCULES

Dimensions: Span, 132 ft 7 in (40,41 m); length, 97 ft 9 in (29,78 m); height, 38 ft 3 in (11,66 m); wing area, 1,745 sq ft (162,12 m²).

LOCKHEED P-3C ORION

Country of Origin: USA.

Type: Long-range maritime patrol aircraft.

Power Plant: Four 4,910 eshp Allison T56-A-14W turbo-props.

Performance: Max. speed at 105,000 lb (47 625 kg), 437 mph (703 km/h) at 15,000 ft (4 570 m); normal cruise, 397 mph (639 km/h) at 25,000 ft (7 620 ml); patrol speed, 230 mph (370 km/h) at 1,500 ft (457 m); loiter endurance (all engines) at 1,500 ft (457 m) 12·3 hours, (two engines), 17 hrs; max. mission radius, 2,530 mls (4 075 km), with 3 hrs on station at 1,500 ft (457 m), 1,933 mls (3 110 km); initial climb, 2,880 ft/min (14,6 m/sec).

Weights: Empty, 62,000 lb (28 123 kg); normal max. take-off, 133,500 lb (60 558 kg); max. overload, 142,000 lb (64 410 kg).

Accommodation: Normal flight crew of 10 of which five housed in tactical compartment. Up to 50 combat troops and 4,000 lb (1 814 kg) of equipment for trooping role.

Armament: Weapons bay can house two Mk 101 depth bombs and four Mk 43, 44 or 46 torpedoes, or eight Mk 54 bombs. External ordnance load of up to 13,713 lb (6 220 kg).

Status: YP-3C prototype flown October 8, 1968, P-3C deliveries commencing to US Navy mid-1969 with 202 programmed of which some 125 delivered by 1975.

Notes: The P-3C differs from the P-3A (157 built) and -3B (144 built) primarily in having more advanced sensor equip-ment. Twelve P-3As have been modified as EP-3Es for the electronic reconnaissance role, others have been adapted for the weather reconnaissance role as WP-3As, and a specially-equipped version, the RP-3D, is being used to map the earth's magnetic field.

LOCKHEED P-3C ORION

Dimensions: Span, 99 ft 8 in (30,37 m); length, 116 ft 10 in (35,61 m); height, 33 ft 8½ in (10,29 m); wing area, 1,300 sq ft (120,77 m²).

LOCKHEED F-104S STARFIGHTER

Country of Origin: USA.

Type: Single-seat interceptor and strike fighter.

Power Plant: One 11,870 lb (5 385 kg) dry and 17,900 lb (8 120 kg) reheat General Electric J79-GE-19 turbojet.

Performance: Max. speed, 910 mph (1 470 km/h) or Mach 1·2 at sea level, 1,450 mph (2 335 km/h) or Mach 2·2 at 36,000 ft (10 970 m); max. cruise, 610 mph (980 km/h) at 36,000 ft (10 970 m); tactical radius with two 162 Imp gal (736 l) and two 100 Imp gal (455 l) drop tanks, 740–775 mls (1 190–1 245 km); ferry range, 1,815 mls (2 920 km); initial climb, 50,000 plus ft/min (254 plus m/sec).

Weights: Empty equipped (interceptor), 15,006 lb (6 807 kg), (strike fighter), 15,761 lb (7 149 kg); loaded (clean), (strike fighter), 21,585 lb (9 791 kg); max. take-off, 31,000 lb (14 060 kg).

Armament: (Interceptor) One 20-mm M-61 rotary cannon, two AIM-7 Sparrow III and two AIM-9 Sidewinder AAMs.

Status: First of two Lockheed-built F-104S prototypes flown December 1966, and first Fiat-built production F-104S flown December 30, 1968. Production of 205 for Italian Air Force with 100th delivered in January 1973, and continuing at rate of two–three per month at beginning of 1975. Deliveries scheduled for completion by early 1976.

Notes: Derivative of the F-104G (see 1966 edition) optimised for all-weather intercept role. Features uprated engine with redesigned afterburner. Nine external stores attachment points. Eighteen aircraft built against Italian Air Force contracts have been diverted to Turkey which country had an option on a further 18 aircraft expiring in March 1975.

124

LOCKHEED F-104S STARFIGHTER

Dimensions: Span, 21 ft 11 in (6,68 m); length, 54 ft 9 in (16,69 m); height, 13 ft 6 in (4,11 m); wing area, 196·1 sq ft (18,22 m²).

LOCKHEED S-3A VIKING

Country of Origin: USA.

Type: Four-seat shipboard anti-submarine aircraft.

Power Plant: Two 9,280 lb (4 210 kg) General Electric TF34-GE-2 turbofans.

Performance: Max. speed, 506 mph (815 km/h) at sea level; max. cruise, 403 mph (649 km/h); typical loiter speed, 184 mph (257 km/h); max. ferry range, 3,500 mls (5 630 km) plus; initial climb, 3,937 ft/min (20 m/sec); service ceiling, 35,000 ft (10 670 m); sea level endurance, 7·5 hrs at 186 mph (300 km/h).

Weights: Empty equipped, 26,554 lb (12 044 kg); normal max. take-off, 43,491 lb (19 727 kg).

Accommodation: Pilot and co-pilot side by side on flight deck, with tactical co-ordinator and sensor operator in aft cabin. All four crew members provided with zero-zero ejection seats.

Armament: Various combinations of torpedoes, depth charges, bombs and ASMs in internal weapons bay and on underwing pylons.

Status: First of eight development and evaluation aircraft commenced its test programme on January 21, 1972, and remaining seven had flown by early 1973. Deliveries against follow-on orders for 138 scheduled for delivery at rate of four per month through 1976. Current US Navy planning calls for acquisition of 179 production aircraft.

Notes: Intended as a successor to the Grumman S-2 Tracker in US Navy service, Lockheed's shipboard turbofan-powered ASW aircraft was selected for development mid-1969 after competitive evaluation of a number of proposals, and entered fleet service during the course of 1974. A stretched version for use as a carrier onboard delivery aircraft will fly as a prototype in 1976.

LOCKHEED S-3A VIKING

Dimensions: Span, 68 ft 8 in (20,93 m); length, 53 ft 4 in (16,26 m); height, 22 ft 9 in (6,93 m); wing area, 598 sq ft (55,56 m²).

McDONNELL DOUGLAS DC-9 SERIES 50

Country of Origin: USA.

Type: Short-to-medium-haul commercial transport.

Power Plant: Two 16,000 lb (7 257 kg) Pratt & Whitney JT8D-17 turbofans.

Performance: Max. cruise, 564 mph (907 km/h) at 27,000 ft (8 230 m); econ. cruise, 535 mph (861 km/h) at 33,000 ft (10 060 m); long-range cruise, 509 mph (819 km/h) at 35,000 ft (10 668 m); range with max. payload (33,000 lb/ 14 950 kg), 1,468 mls (2 362 km), with max. fuel (and 21,400-lb/9 700-kg payload), 2,787 mls (4 485 km).

Weights: Operational empty, 65,000 lb (29 484 kg); max. take-off, 120,000 lb (54 430 kg).

Accommodation: Flight crew of two/three and maximum high-density arrangement for 139 passengers in five-abreast seating.

Status: The first DC-9 Series 50 was scheduled to fly during January 1975 with first delivery (against initial order for 10 from Swissair) following during July 1975. Twenty-six firm orders for the Series 50 had been received by the beginning of 1975.

Notes: The latest of five basic DC-9 models, the Series 50 represents a further "stretch" of the basic DC-9 airframe, the fuselage being 6·4 ft (1,95 m) longer than the previously largest DC-9, the Series 40. The DC-9 was first flown on February 25, 1965, and the 700th aircraft of this type was delivered in July 1973. Production versions include the initial Series 10, the Series 20 (see 1969 edition) retaining the short fuselage of the Series 10 with the longer-span wing of the Series 30 (see 1973 edition) and the Series 40 (see 1972 edition). The Series 60 is projected with a further fuselage "stretch" and refanned engines.

McDONNELL DOUGLAS DC-9 SERIES 50

Dimensions: Span, 93 ft 5 in (28,47 m); length, 132 ft 0 in (40,23 m); height, 27 ft 6 in (8,38 m); wing area, 1,000·7 sq ft (92,97 m²).

McDONNELL DOUGLAS DC-10 SERIES 30

Country of Origin: USA.

Type: Medium-range commercial transport.

Power Plant: Three 51,000 lb (23 134 kg) General Electric CF6-50C turbofans.

Performance: Max. cruise (at 520,000 lb/235 868 kg), 570 mph (917 km/h) at 31,000 ft (9 450 m); long-range cruise, 554 mph (891 km/h) at 31,000 ft (9 450 m); max. fuel range (with 230 mls/370 km reserves), 6,909 mls (11 118 km); max. payload range, 4,272 mls (6 875 km); max. climb rate, 2,320 ft/min (11,78 m/sec); service ceiling (at 540,000 lb/244 940 kg), 32,700 ft (9 965 m).

Weights: Basic operating, 263,087 lb (119 334 kg); max. take-off, 555,000 lb (251 745 kg).

Accommodation: Flight crew of three plus provision on flight deck for two supernumerary crew. Typical mixed-class accommodation for 225–270 passengers. Max. authorised passenger accommodation, 380 (plus crew of 11).

Status: First DC-10 (Series 10) flown August 29, 1970, with first Series 30 (46th DC-10 built) flying June 21, 1972, being preceded on February 28, 1972, by first Series 40. Orders totalled 229 by December 1974, a total of 51 being delivered during the course of that year.

Notes: The DC-10 Series 30 and 40 have identical fuselages to the DC-10 Series 10 (see 1972 edition), but whereas the last-mentioned version is a domestic model, the Series 30 and 40 are intercontinental models, and differ in power plant, weight and wing details, and in the use of three main undercarriage units, the third (a twin-wheel unit) being mounted on the fuselage centreline.

McDONNELL DOUGLAS DC-10 SERIES 30

Dimensions: Span, 165 ft 4 in (50,42 m); length, 181 ft 4¾ in (55,29 m); height, 58 ft 0 in (17,68 m); wing area, 3,921·4 sq ft (364,3 m²).

McDONNELL DOUGLAS F-15 EAGLE

Country of Origin: USA.

Type: Single-seat air-superiority fighter.

Power Plant: Two (approx.) 19,000 lb (8 618 kg) dry and 27,000 lb (12 247 kg) reheat Pratt & Whitney F100-PW-101 turbofans.

Performance: Max. sustained speed (approx.), 1,520 mph (2 446 km/h) or Mach 2·3 above 36,000 ft (10 975 m); max. short-period dash speed, 1,650 mph (2 655 km/h) or Mach 2·5; max. low-altitude speed (approx.), 915 mph (1 470 km/h) or Mach 1·2 at 1,000 ft (305 m); max. endurance (with Fast Pack fuel pallets), 5·5 hrs.

Weights: Approx. max. loaded (air superiority mission), 40,000 lb (18 144 kg); max. take-off, 56,000 lb (25 400 kg).

Armament: One 20-mm M-61A-1 rotary cannon (eventually to be replaced by a 25-mm Philco-Ford GAU-7/A rotary cannon) and mix of four Raytheon AIM-7F Sparrow and four Raytheon AIM-9L Sidewinder AAMs.

Status: First of 20 development and test Eagles flown on July 27, 1972, with second and third following on September 26 and November 4, 1972, respectively. Eight of these 20 aircraft were being used during 1973–74 for service evaluation and 12 for the contractor's test programme. The first production Eagle (a TF-15) flew on September 25, 1974. The Eagle is entering the USAF inventory during 1975 and current planning calls for the purchase of 729 fighters of this type. Production rate was 6–7 per month at beginning of 1975.

Notes: Intended to provide the USAF with its principal air superiority capability during the period 1975–85, the Eagle is allegedly capable of climbing vertically at supersonic speed and of accelerating from subsonic cruise to speed of the order of Mach 1·5 within less than one minute. A tandem two-seat version is designated TF-15.

132

McDONNELL DOUGLAS F-15 EAGLE

Dimensions: Span, 42 ft 9½ in (13,04 m); length, 63 ft 9½ in (19,44 m); height, 18 ft 7¼ in (5,67 m).

McDONNELL DOUGLAS F-4 PHANTOM

Country of Origin: USA.

Type: Two-seat interceptor and tactical strike fighter.

Power Plant: Two 11,870 lb (5 385 kg) dry and 17,900 lb (8 120 kg) reheat General Electric J79-GE-17 or (F-4F) MTU-built J79-MTU-17A turbojets.

Performance: (F-4E) Max. speed without external stores, 910 mph (1 464 km/h) or Mach 1·2 at 1,000 ft (305 m), 1,500 mph (2 414 km/h) or Mach 2·27 at 40,000 ft (12 190 m); tactical radius (with four Sparrow III and four Sidewinder AAMs), 140 mls (225 km), (plus one 500 Imp gal/2 273 l auxiliary tank), 196 mls (315 km), (hi-lo-hi mission profile with four 1,000-lb/453,6-kg bombs, four AAMs, and one 500 Imp gal/2 273 l and two 308 Imp gal/1 400 l tanks), 656 mls (1 056 km); max. ferry range, 2,300 mls (3 700 km) at 575 mph (925 km/h).

Weights: (F-4E) Empty equipped, 30,425 lb (13 801 kg); loaded (with four Sparrow IIIs), 51,810 lb (21 500 kg), (plus four Sidewinders and max. external fuel), 58,000 lb (26 308 kg); max. overload, 60,630 lb (27 502 kg).

Armament: One 20-mm M-61A1 rotary cannon and (intercept) four or six AIM-7E plus four AIM-9D AAMs, or (attack) up to 16,000 lb (7 257 kg) of external stores.

Status: First F-4E flown June 1967, and production continuing at beginning of 1974. First F-4F (for Federal Germany) completed May 1973 with deliveries through 1974. Phantom deliveries exceeded 4,500 by the beginning of 1975 when the backlog was some 400 aircraft and production rate was 18 per month.

Notes: Current production models of the Phantom in addition to the F-4E (see 1973 edition) are the RF-4E (see 1972 edition), the F-4EJ for Japan and the F-4F for Federal Germany. The last-mentioned version (illustrated on opposite page), optimised for the intercept role, entered service with the Luftwaffe from January 1, 1974, and features leading-edge slats and various weight-saving features.

McDONNELL DOUGLAS F-4 PHANTOM

Dimensions: Span, 38 ft $4\frac{3}{4}$ in (11,70 m); length, 62 ft $10\frac{1}{2}$ in (19,20 m); height, 16 ft $3\frac{1}{3}$ in (4,96 m); wing area, 530 sq ft (49,2 m²).

McDONNELL DOUGLAS A-4N SKYHAWK II

Country of Origin: USA.

Type: Single-seat light attack bomber.

Power Plant: One 11,200 lb (5 080 kg) Pratt & Whitney J52-P-408A turbojet.

Performance: Max. speed without external stores, 685 mph (1 102 km/h) or Mach 0·9 at sea level, 640 mph (1 030 km/h) at 25,000 ft (7 620 m), in high drag configuration, 625 mph (1 080 km/h) or Mach 0·82 at sea level, 605 mph (973 km/h) or Mach 0·84 at 30,000 ft (9 145 m); combat radius on internal fuel for hi-lo-lo-hi mission profile with 4,000 lb (1 814 kg) of external stores, 340 mls (547 km); initial climb, 15,850 ft/min (80,5 m/sec), at 23,000 lb (10 433 kg), 8,440 ft/min (42,7 m/sec).

Weights: Empty, 10,600 lb (4 808 kg); max. take-off, 24,500 lb (11 113 kg).

Armament: Two 30-mm DEFA cannon and external weapons loads up to 8,200 lb (3 720 kg) on wing and fuselage hardpoints.

Status: First A-4N flown June 12, 1972, with first production deliveries (to Israel) initiated November 1972.

Notes: The A-4N employs essentially the same power plant and airframe as the A-4M (see 1972 edition), both models being referred to as the Skyhawk II. The A-4N embodies some of the features originally developed for the Israeli A-4H (e.g., twin 30-mm cannon) but has a new nav/attack system (similar to A-7D and -7E) and a revised cockpit layout. Thirty-six A-4M Skyhawks were ordered by Kuwait late 1974.

McDONNELL DOUGLAS A-4N SKYHAWK II

Dimensions: Span, 27 ft 6 in (8,38 m); length, 40 ft 3$\frac{1}{4}$ in (12,27 m); height, 15 ft 0 in (4,57 m); wing area, 260 sq ft (24,16 m²).

MIKOYAN MIG-21SMT (FISHBED-K)

Country of Origin: USSR.

Type: Single-seat multi-purpose fighter.

Power Plant: One 11,244 lb (5 100 kg) dry and 14,550 lb (6 600 kg) reheat Tumansky R-13 turbojet.

Performance: Max. speed, 808 mph (1 300 km/h) at 1,000 ft (305 m) or Mach 1·06, 1,386 mph (2 230 km/h) above 36,090 ft (11 000 m) or Mach 2·1; approx. range on internal fuel, 750 mls (1 207 km); endurance (with one centreline drop tank), 3·5 hrs; service ceiling, 59,055 ft (18 000 m).

Weights: Approx. normal take-off (with four K-13 AAMs), 18,500 lb (8 392 kg); approx. max. take-off, 21,000 lb (9 525 kg).

Armament: One twin-barrel 23-mm GSh-23 cannon with 200 rounds and up to four AAMs (Atoll and Advanced Atoll) on wing pylons for intercept role. Various external stores for ground attack, including UV-16-57 or UV-32-57 pods each containing 16 and 32 55-mm S-5 rockets respectively, 240-mm S-24 rockets or 550-lb (250-kg) bombs.

Status: The MiG-21SMT is a progressive development of the MiG-21MF (see 1974 edition) and began to enter service with the Soviet Air Forces in 1973.

Notes: Referred to as the "third generation" MiG-21, the MiG-21SMT differs from the MiG-21MF primarily in having revised upper fuselage contours resulting from the introduction of a "saddle" fuel tank to improve the previously inadequate range and endurance on internal fuel, leaving the wing pylons free for ordnance. The MiG-21SMT also reportedly features upgraded avionics.

MIKOYAN MIG-21SMT (FISHBED-K)

Dimensions: Span, 23 ft 5½ in (7,15 m); length (including probe), 51 ft 8½ in (15,76 m), (without probe), 44 ft 2 in (13,46 m); wing area, 247.57 sq ft (23,0 m²).

MIKOYAN MIG-23B (FLOGGER-B)

Country of Origin: USSR.

Type: Single-seat multi-role fighter.

Power Plant: One 14,330 lb (6 500 kg) dry and 20,500 lb (9 300 kg) reheat Tumansky turbojet.

Performance: (Estimated) Max. speed, 865 mph at 1,000 ft (305 m) or Mach 1·2, 1,520 mph (2 446 km/h) above 39,370 ft (12 000 m) or Mach 2·3, (high drag configuration —centreline fuel tank and four AAMs), 1,120 mph (1 800 km/h) above 39,370 ft (12 000 m) or Mach 1·7; tactical radius (with centreline drop tank), 620 mls (1 000 km).

Weights: Approx. max. take-off, 33,070 lb (15 000 kg).

Armament: One 23-mm twin-barrel GSh-23 cannon and various external ordnance loads (e.g. four AAMs) on two fuselage pylons and two pylons on fixed wing centre section.

Status: The MiG-23B is believed to have entered service during 1971, and during the course of 1974 was exported to Iraq and Syria.

Notes: The MiG-23 multi-role fighter is currently in service in both single-seat (Flogger-B) and two-seat (Flogger-C) versions, the latter have a dual conversion training/operational role.

MIKOYAN MIG-23B (FLOGGER-B)

Dimensions: (Estimated) Span (max.), 46 ft 9 in (14,25 m), (min.), 26 ft 9½ in (8,17 m); length, 55 ft 1½ in (16,80 m).

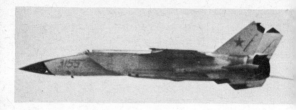

MIKOYAN MIG-25 (FOXBAT)

Country of Origin: USSR.

Type: Single-seat interceptor (Foxbat A) and reconnaissance fighter (Foxbat B).

Power Plant: Two (approx.) 24,250 lb (11 000 kg) reheat Tumansky turbojets.

Performance: (Estimated) Max. short-period dash speed, 2,100 mph (3 380 km/h) or Mach 3·2 at 39,370 ft (12 000 m); max. sustained speed, 1,780 mph (2 865 km/h) or Mach 2·7 at 39,370 ft (12 000 m), 975 mph (1 570 km/h) or Mach 1·3 at 4,920 ft (1 500 m); normal combat radius, 700 mls (1 125 km); time to 36,000 ft (10 970 m), 2·5 min.

Weights: (Estimated) Empty equipped, 34,000 lb (15 420 kg); normal loaded, 50,000–55,000 lb (22 680–24 950 kg); max. take-off, 64,200 lb (29 120 kg).

Armament: Four wing stations for radar homing AAMs for the intercept role. The MiG-25R (Foxbat B) has camera nose and no weapons pylons.

Status: Believed flown in prototype form 1963–64 with service deliveries following from 1970–71.

Notes: The MiG-25 multi-purpose fighter has established a number of FAI-recognised records since 1965 under the designation Ye-266. During 1973, the Ye-266 averaged, 1,619 mph (2 605 km/h) over a 100-km closed circuit, attained an altitude of 98,425 ft (30 000 m) in 4 min 3·9 sec, and established an absolute altitude record of 118,897 ft (36 240 m). The MiG-25 has *Jay Bird* (J-band) radar for missile guidance and target location, and it is equipped to receive signals from a ground-to-air digital transmission system incorporating ground-based tracking radars. The MiG-25R has performed reconnaissance missions at extreme altitudes over Israel from Egyptian bases.

MIKOYAN MIG-25 (FOXBAT)

Dimensions: (Estimated) Span, 41 ft 0 in (12,5 m); length, 70 ft 0 in (21,33 m).

MITSUBISHI MU-2L

Country of Origin: Japan.

Type: Light business executive and utility transport.

Power Plant: Two 776 eshp Garrett AiResearch TPE-331 turboprops.

Performance: Max. cruise, 345 mph (555 km/h) at 15,000 ft (4 572 m); econ. cruise, 304 mph (490 km/h) at 25,000 ft (7 620 m); max. range with 45 min reserves, 1,462 mls (2 350 km) at 22,965 ft (7 000 m); initial climb, 2,697 ft/ min (13,7 m/sec); service ceiling, 30,775 ft (9 380 m).

Weights: Empty equipped, 7,000 lb (3 175 kg); max. take-off, 11,575 lb (5 250 kg).

Accommodation: Normal flight crew of two and various cabin arrangements providing accommodation for four to a maximum of 12 passengers.

Status: The MU-2L was introduced in September 1974 as a successor to the lower-powered MU-2J (see 1974 edition). A parallel civil model is the MU-2M. Production of MU-2s of all versions was approaching 400 aircraft by 1975.

Notes: The MU-2L and MU-2M are follow-on models of the MU-2J and MU-2K respectively, the MU-2M differing from the MU-2L in having a shorter overall length (33 ft 2¾ in/ 10,13 m) and mainwheels retracting into the fuselage rather than into side fairings. The MU-2L and M have uprated engines, higher weights, new oleos and undercarriage retraction mechanism and new wing flaps.

MITSUBISHI MU-2L

Dimensions: Span, 39 ft 2 in (11,95 m); length, 39 ft 5¾ in (12,03 m); height, 13 ft 8¼ in (4,17 m); wing area, 178 sq ft (16,55 m²).

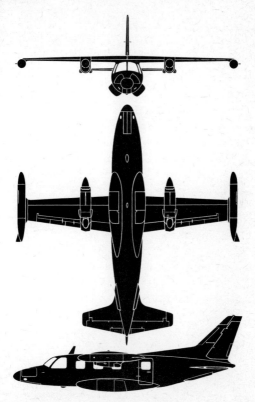

MITSUBISHI T-2

Country of Origin: Japan.

Type: Tandem two-seat advanced trainer.

Power Plant: Two 3,810 lb (1 728 kg) dry and 7,070 lb (3 207 kg) reheat Ishikawajima-Harima-built Rolls-Royce Turboméca RB.172-T.260 Adour turbofans.

Performance: (Estimated) Max. speed, 1,056 mph (1 700 km/h) or Mach 1·6 at 40,000 ft (12 190 m); max. ferry range, 1,600 mls (2 575 km); max. climb rate, 35,100 ft/min (178 m/sec); service ceiling, 50,000 ft (15 240 m).

Weights: Empty, 13,662 lb (6 197 kg); loaded (clean) 21,325 lb (9 673 kg); max. 28,220 lb (12 800 kg).

Armament: One 20-mm M-61 rotary cannon internally and various external ordnance loads on fuselage, underwing, and wingtip stations for combat training role.

Status: First of four flying prototypes was flown on July 20, 1971. Current plans call for deliveries of 59 production T-2A trainers, the first production aircraft having been scheduled to fly in January 1975 with completion of deliveries by late 1978.

Notes: Japan's first indigenous supersonic aircraft, the T-2A trainer is intended to enter the inventory of the Air Self-Defence Force late 1975. The basic design is also intended to fulfil operational roles, and the ASDF is to receive 68 examples of a close-support fighter version, the FS-T2Kai, these entering the inventory from 1977 onwards. A single-seater, the FS-T2Kai will carry a 20-mm rotary cannon and eight 500-lb (227-kg) bombs, two ASM-1 anti-shipping missiles or 12 500-lb (227-kg) bombs in overload condition. Max. take-off weight will be 30,865 lb (14 000 kg).

MITSUBISHI T-2

Dimensions: Span, 25 ft 11 in (7,90 m); length, 58 ft 4¾ in (17,80 m); height, 14 ft 9¼ in (4,50 m); wing area, 228·2 sq ft (21,2 m²).

NORTHROP F-5E TIGER II

Country of Origin: USA.

Type: Single-seat air-superiority fighter.

Power Plant: Two 3,500 lb (1 588 kg) dry and 5,000 lb (2 268 kg) reheat General Electric J85-GE-21 turbojets.

Performance: Max. speed (at 13,220 lb/5 997 kg), 1056 mph (1 700 km/h) or Mach 1·6 at 36,090 ft (11 000 m), 760 mph (1 223 km/h) or Mach 1·0 at sea level, (with wing-tip missiles), 990 mph (1 594 km/h) or Mach 1·5 at 36,090 ft (11 000 m); combat radius (internal fuel), 173 mls (278 km), (with 229 Imp gal/1 041 l drop tank), 426 mls (686 km); initial climb (at 13,220 lb/5 997 kg), 31,600 ft/min (160,53 m/sec); combat ceiling, 53,500 ft (16 305 m).

Weights: Take-off (wingtip launching rail configuration), 15,400 lb (6 985 kg); max. take-off, 24,083 lb (10 924 kg).

Armament: Two 20-mm M-39 cannon with 280 rpg and two wingtip-mounted AIM-9 Sidewinder AAMs. Up to 7,000 lb (3 175 kg) of ordnance (for attack role).

Status: First F-5E flown August 11, 1972, and first deliveries February 1973. Forty-eight delivered during 1973, followed by 158 in 1974, and 250 being scheduled for delivery in 1975, production tempo reaching 20 per month by mid-year.

Notes: A more powerful derivative of the F-5A (see 1970 edition) optimised for the air-superiority role, the F-5E won the USAF's International Fighter Aircraft (IFA) contest in November 1970, and is being supplied under the Military Assistance Programme to South Korea, South Vietnam, Taiwan, Thailand and Jordan. Orders for the F-5E have also been placed by Brazil, Chile, Iran, Saudi Arabia and Malaysia. The two-seat F-5F flew on September 25, 1974.

NORTHROP F-5E TIGER II

Dimensions: Span, 26 ft 8½ in (8,14 m); length, 48 ft 2½ in (14,69 m); height, 13 ft 4 in (4,06 m); wing area, 186·2 sq ft (17,29 m²).

NORTHROP YF-17

Country of Origin: USA.

Type: Single-seat air superiority fighter.

Power Plant: Two (approx.) 15,000 lb (6 804 kg) reheat General Electric YJ101-GE-100 turbojets.

Performance: Estimated max. speed, 835 mph (1 344 km/h) at 1,000 ft (305 m) or Mach 1·1, 1,450 mph (2 333 km/h) above 36,000 ft (10 970 m) or Mach 2·2; approx. combat radius (internal fuel), 550 mls (885 km); max. ferry range (with external fuel), 2,990 mls (4 810 km); absolute ceiling, 65,000 ft (19 810 m).

Weights: Normal take-off (including two AIM-9 Sidewinder AAMs and full internal fuel), 23,000 lb (10 433 kg); approx. max. take-off, 38,000 lb (17 237 kg).

Armament: One 20-mm M-61A Vulcan rotary cannon and (intercept role), two AIM-9 Sidewinder AAMs.

Status: First of two prototypes flown June 9, 1974, with second following on August 21, 1974.

Notes: Although intended originally as a lightweight fighter technology development aircraft essentially similar to the company-funded P-530 Cobra multi-purpose fighter project, the YF-17 (which has the company designation P-600) participated in a competitive fly-off with the General Dynamics YF-16 (see pages 86–87) for selection as the basis of the USAF's ACF (Air Combat Fighter) during 1974, the result of this fly-off having been scheduled for early 1975. At the beginning of 1975, it was envisaged that the USAF would receive approximately 650 ACF aircraft based on the design of the winning contender, with deliveries commencing in 1978 and initial operational status being achieved during the following year.

NORTHROP YF-17

Dimensions: Span, 35 ft 0 in (10,67 m); length (excluding nose probe), 56 ft 0 in (17,07 m); height, 14 ft 6 in (4,42 m); wing area, 350 sq ft (32,51 m²).

NZAI CT-4 AIRTRAINER

Country of Origin: New Zealand.

Type: Side-by-side two-seat primary trainer.

Power Plant: One 210 hp Continental IO-360-D six-cylinder horizontally-opposed engine.

Performance: Max. speed, 183 mph (294 km/h) at sea level, 168 mph (270 km/h) at 10,000 ft (3 048 m); cruise (75% power), 158 mph (254 km/h) at sea level, 144 mph (232 km/h) at 10,000 ft (3 048 m), (55% power), 138 mph (222 km/h) at sea level; max. range (at 65% power), 824 mls (1 326 km) at 135 mph (217 km/h) at 5,000 ft (1 524 m), (with two 17·5 Imp gal/79,5 l wingtip tanks), 1,400 mls (2 253 km) at 5,000 ft (1 524 m); initial climb, 1,345 ft/min (6,8 m/sec).

Weights: Empty equipped, 1,520 lb (690 kg); design max. take-off, 2,350 lb (1 070 kg), (with tip tanks), 2,650 lb (1 202 kg).

Status: Prototype flown February 21, 1972, with first production (to Royal Thai Air Force) October 1973. First aircraft for the R.A.A.F. was scheduled to be delivered in January 1975.

Notes: Manufactured by New Zealand Aerospace Industries (NZAI) formed in 1973 by the amalgamation of Aero Engine Services and Air Parts (NZ), the CT-4 has been ordered by the Royal Thai Air Force (24), by the Royal Australian Air Force (37), by the Royal New Zealand Air Force (13) and by the Royal Hong Kong Auxiliary Air Force (three).

NZAI CT-4 AIRTRAINER

Dimensions: Span, 26 ft 0 in (7,92 m); length, 23 ft 2 in (7,06 m); height, 8 ft 6 in (2,59 m); wing area, 129 sq ft (12,00 m²).

PANAVIA MRCA

Countries of Origin: UK, Federal Germany and Italy.

Type: Two-seat multi-purpose fighter.

Power Plant: Two 8,500 lb (3 855 kg) dry and 14,500 lb (6 577 kg) reheat Turbo Union RB.199-34R turbofans.

Performance: Max. speed, 1,320+ mph (2 125+ km/h) above 36,000 ft (10 970 m) or Mach 2·0+; estimated combat endurance on internal fuel, 70–80 min.

Weights: Empty equipped, 22,000–23,000 lb (9 980–10 430 kg); max. take-off, 38,000–40,000 lb (17 240–18 145 kg).

Armament: Two 27-mm Mauser cannon internally-mounted and various ordnance combinations on three fuselage and four swivelling wing pylons.

Status: First of nine prototype and pre-production aircraft, the P.01, flown on August 14, 1974, followed by the second, P.02, on October 30, and the third, P.03, was scheduled to fly in January 1975 and will be followed by P.04 during the following summer. Three, P.01, 04 and 07, are being assembled in Germany, four, P.02, 03, 05 and 08, are being assembled in the UK, and two, P.05 and P.09, in Italy. Current planning calls for the production of 322 MRCAs for the *Luftwaffe* and *Marineflieger*, 385 for the RAF and approximately 100 for Italy's *Aeronautica Militare*. Production deliveries to the RAF will commence 1978–79.

Notes: The MRCA (multi-role combat aircraft) is being developed by Panavia, a multi-national European company, basically for the strike role, but an interceptor version is to be developed for the RAF for operation from the early 'eighties, and some 25–30 per cent of the MRCAs to be acquired by the RAF will be of this version.

PANAVIA MRCA

Dimensions: Span (max.), 45 ft 7 in (13,90 m), (min.), 28 ft 2½ in (8,60 m); length, 54 ft 10 in (16,70 m); height, 18 ft 8½ in (5,70 m).

PARTENAVIA P.68B VICTOR

Country of Origin: Italy.
Type: Light utility and business executive aircraft.
Power Plant: Two 200 hp Lycoming IO-360-A1B four-cylinder horizontally-opposed engines.
Performance: Max. speed, 200 mph (322 km/h) at sea level; cruise at 75% power, 190 mph (306 km/h) at 5,500 ft (1 675 m), at 65% power, 184 mph (296 km/h) at 9,000 ft (2 745 m); range (pilot and four passengers) at 75% power, 982 mls (1 580 km), at 65% power, 1,056 mls (1 700 km); initial climb, 1,600 ft/min (8,13 m/sec); service ceiling, 20,000 ft (6 096 m).
Weights: Empty, 2,645 lb (1 200 kg); max. take-off, 4,321 lb (1 960 kg).
Accommodation: Seating for pilot and five passengers in side-by-side pairs. Dual controls standard.
Status: First prototype P.68 flown on May 25, 1970, followed by 13 pre-production aircraft, all of which had been completed by early 1974, when, after transfer to a new factory, production continued with the P.68B, six having been completed by mid-year. Production rate of three–four per month by beginning of 1975.
Notes: The P.68B differs from the original P.68 (see 1973 edition) primarily in having a 6-in (15-cm) extension in the fuselage just aft of the cockpit, improved instrumentation and an increase in gross weight. Certification of a version with a retractable undercarriage is scheduled during the course of 1975, and it is anticipated that versions of the P.68 will be offered with either 180 or 200 hp engines and either fixed or retractable undercarriages.

156

PARTENAVIA P.68B VICTOR

Dimensions: Span, 39 ft 4½ in (12,00 m); length, 30 ft 8 in (9,35 m); height, 11 ft 2 in (3,40 m); wing area, 200·2 sq ft (18,60 m²).

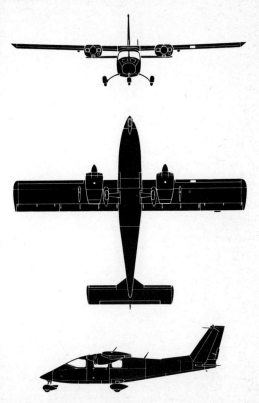

PIPER PA-31T CHEYENNE

Country of Origin: USA.

Type: Light business executive transport.

Power Plant: Two 620 shp UACL PT6A-28A turboprops.

Performance: Max. speed, 283 mph (455 km/h) at sea level, 321 mph (517 km/h) at optimum altitude; max. cruise, 302 mph (486 km/h) at 20,000 ft (6 096 m); normal cruise, 276 mph (444 km/h) at 20,000 ft (6 096 m); max. range, 1,638 mls (2 640 km); range at max. cruise (with 800-lb/363-kg payload), 1,407 mls (2 260 km); range with 3,200-lb (1 451-kg) payload, 235 mls (378 km); initial climb, 2,800 ft/min (14,2 m/sec).

Weights: Empty, 4,870 lb (2 210 kg); typical empty equipped, 5,420 lb (2 458 kg); max. take-off, 9,000 lb (4 082 kg).

Accommodation: Side-by-side seating for pilot and co-pilot/passenger and seating arrangements for four–six passengers.

Status: Prototype flown in 1969 but decision to proceed with production not taken until 1973, with first customer delivery on March 27, 1974. Planned production rate of 12 aircraft per month in 1975.

Notes: The first turboprop-powered business executive aircraft to be produced in series by Piper, the Cheyenne is essentially a re-engined and refined derivative of the PA-31P Pressurised Navajo, current members of the Navajo range comprising the PA-31-310 (see 1972 edition), the PA-31-350 Navajo Chieftain (see 1973 edition) and PA-31P-425.

PIPER PA-31T CHEYENNE

Dimensions: Span, 42 ft 8 in (13,00 m); length, 34 ft 8 in (10,57 m); height, 12 ft 9 in (3,88 m); wing area, 229 sq ft (21,27 m²).

POLIGRAT MASTER PORTER PD-01

Country of Origin: Federal Germany (and Switzerland).
Type: Light STOL utility transport.
Power Plant: Two 1,120 shp UACL PT6A-45 turboprops.
Performance: (Estimated) Max. speed, 265 mph (426 km/h) at 10,000 ft (3 050 m); normal cruise, 249 mph (400 km/h); econ. cruise, 201 mph (324 km/h); range (max. fuel), 1,490 mls (2 400 km), (max. payload), 124 mls (200 km); initial climb, 2,380 ft/min (12,1 m/sec); service ceiling, 28,000 ft (8 500 m).
Weights: Empty, 7,238 lb (3 290 kg); max. take-off, 14,330 lb (6 500 kg).
Accommodation: Flight crew of two and 19 passengers in three-abreast seating or 24 in four-abreast seating. In the freighter role, 88-in (2,24-m) pallets or LD-1, LD-3 or LD-7 containers may be accommodated.
Status: Two prototypes built under contract by Pilatus of Stans, Switzerland, scheduled to fly during course of 1975.
Notes: Designed by Poligrat Development of Munich which has contracted with Pilatus for the construction of two prototypes, a static test specimen, and manufacture of tooling for an initial production batch, the Master Porter has been developed primarily for licence manufacture in countries with spare production capacity and a promising potential market.

POLIGRAT MASTER PORTER PD-01

Dimensions: Span, 57 ft 1 in (17,40 m); length, 45 ft 3 in (13,79 m); height, 20 ft 8 in (6,30 m); wing area, 408·5 sq ft (37,94 m²).

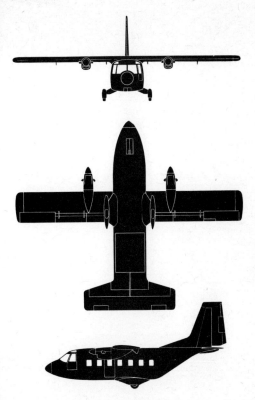

PZL-106 KRUK

Country of Origin: Poland.

Type: Single-seat agricultural monoplane.

Power Plant: One 400 hp Avco Lycoming IO-720-A1B eight-cylinder horizontally-opposed engine.

Performance: Max. speed, 130 mph (210 km/h); econ. cruise, 106 mph (170 km/h); operating speed, 75–99 mph (120–160 km/h); initial climb, 886 ft/min (4,5 m/sec).

Weights: Empty, 2,315 lb (1 050 kg); take-off, 4,762 lb (2 160 kg); max., 4,960 lb (2 250 kg).

Status: First of three prototypes flown on April 17, 1973, with production deliveries scheduled to commence during 1975.

Notes: The PZL-106 Kruk (Raven) is the result of protracted development, project studies stretching back to the early 'sixties and the PZL-101M Kruk project, an extensively re-designed agricultural variant of the PZL-101 Gawron (Rook). Design studies originally centred on the use of the 260 hp Ivchenko AI-14R air-cooled radial, but choice of the Lycoming unit for the initial model was taken in 1972. However, the Kruk has been designed to take a variety of horizontally-opposed or radial piston engines or turboprops in the 360–600 shp range, and the study of versions employing the indigenous K-5 radial (currently rated at 323 hp) and other engines was continuing at the beginning of 1975, the third prototype having been tested with a pre-series K-5 seven-cylinder radial during the course of 1974. The Kruk can accommodate a maximum chemical load of 2,205 lb (1 000 kg).

PZL-106 KRUK

Dimensions: Span, 42 ft $7\frac{7}{8}$ in (13,00 m); length, 27 ft $6\frac{3}{4}$ in (8,40 m); height, 9 ft 6 in (2,90 m); wing area, 317·53 sq ft (29,50 m²).

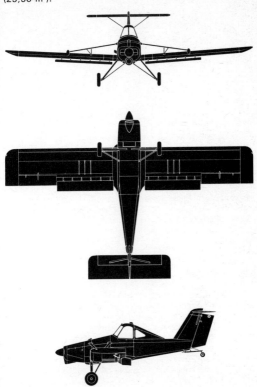

ROCKWELL INTERNATIONAL B-1A

Country of Origin: USA.

Type: Strategic bomber.

Power Plant: Four (approx.) 30,000 lb (13 610 kg) General Electric F101-GE-100 turbofans.

Performance: (Estimated) Max. speed, 1,450 mph (2 335 km/h) at 40,000 ft (12 190 m) or Mach 2·2, 900 mph (1 450 km/h) at 1,500 ft (460 m) or Mach 1·2, 648 mph (1 042 km/h) at sea level or Mach 0·85; typical mission radius (at Mach 0·8) 3,600 mls (5 795 km); max. (unrefuelled) range, 6,100 mls (9 820 km).

Weights: Max. take-off, 389,800 lb (176 822 kg).

Armament: Twenty-four Boeing AGM-69A SRAM (Short Range Attack Missile) ASMs in three weapons bays or equivalent nuclear or conventional bombs plus additional eight SRAM ASMs on two external hard points.

Status: First of three prototypes was rolled out on October 26, 1974, and was scheduled to commence its flight test programme in December 1974 with third (avionics test) prototype flying in late 1975 and preceding second prototype scheduled to join test programme mid-1976. Production decision expected to be taken late 1975 with initial deliveries to USAF Strategic Air Command in 1978.

Notes: Comparable with the Soviet Backfire (see pages 200–201), the B-1A is intended as a successor to the B-52.

164

ROCKWELL INTERNATIONAL B-1A

Dimensions: Span (max.), 136 ft 8½ in (41,66 m), (min.), 78 ft 2½ in (23,83 m); length, 150 ft 2½ in (45,80 m); height, 33 ft 7¼ in (10,24 m).

ROCKWELL XFV-12A

Country of Origin: USA.

Type: Technology development aircraft for single-seat shipboard V/STOL fighter.

Power Plant: One 14,070 lb (6 382 kg) Pratt & Witney F401-PW-400 turbofan (thrust boosted to 21,800 lb/9 888 kg for lift by augmentation system).

Performance: Estimated max. speed, 1,450 mph (2 330 km/h) at 40,000 ft (12 190 m) or Mach 2·2; operational radius (with max. fuel after 300 ft/91 m take-off roll), 575 plus mls (925 plus km).

Weights: Empty, 13,800 lb (6 260 kg); VTO take-off, 19,500 lb (8 845 kg); STO (300 ft/91 m) take-off, 24,250 lb (11 000 kg).

Armament: (Proposed) One 20-mm M-61 rotary cannon on fuselage centreline and four AIM-7 Sparrow AAMs or two AIM-7 and two AIM-9L Sidewinder AAMs.

Status: First of two prototypes is expected to fly during the second half of 1975.

Notes: The XFV-12A is an advanced technology prototype for a projected V/STOL fighter for use from the US Navy's proposed Sea Control Ships and utilising the TAW (Thrust-Augmented Wing) principle, this integrated lift/propulsion/control system facilitating conversion from hover to speeds in excess of Mach 2·0. The exhaust air from the turbofan is ducted to ejector flaps in the canard surfaces and wings, primary and ambient air being mixed and resulting in an augmentation ratio of 1·55. Hovering control is achieved by varying the diffuser geometry of each of the four lifting augmenters. To expedite the development programme, the XFV-12As utilise the A-4 Skyhawk forward fuselage and undercarriage and the F-4 Phantom wing box and air intakes.

ROCKWELL XFV-12A

Dimensions: Span, 28 ft 6 in (8,68 m); length, 43 ft 10 in (13,36 m); height, 9 ft 5 in (2,87 m).

ROCKWELL COMMANDER 112A

Country of Origin: USA.

Type: Light cabin monoplane.

Power Plant: One 200 hp Avco Lycoming IO-360-C1D6 four-cylinder horizontally-opposed engine.

Performance: Max. speed, 171 mph (275 km/h) at sea level; cruise at 75% power at optimum altitude, 161 mph (259 km/h); range at 75% power (45 min reserves at 45% power), 880 mls (1 416 km); optimum range, 975 mls (1 569 km); initial climb, 1,000 ft/min (5,08 m/sec); service ceiling, 13,900 ft (4 337 m).

Weights: Empty, 1,688 lb (766 kg); max. take-off, 2,650 lb (1 202 kg).

Accommodation: Pilot and three passengers seated in pairs with individual seats forward and bench seat aft.

Status: The first of five prototypes was flown on December 4, 1970, and customer deliveries commenced late 1972. The Model 112A was introduced as a successor to the Model 112 in January 1974, deliveries averaging 12 per month during the course of the year.

Notes: The development programme of the Commander 112 was somewhat protracted owing to modifications to the tail assembly necessitated by the loss of a prototype during high-speed diving trials. FAA certification being obtained during the course of 1972. The parallel Commander 111A (see 1972 edition) featured a fixed undercarriage and a 180 hp Lycoming O-360-A1G6 engine driving a constant-speed airscrew, but production is currently concentrated on the improved Commander 112A. A twin-engined version of the basic design and a six-seat version are projected.

ROCKWELL COMMANDER 112A

Dimensions: Span, 32 ft 9 in (9,98 m); length, 24 ft 11 in (7,59 m); height, 8 ft 5 in (2,51 m); wing area, 152 sq ft (14,12 m²).

ROCKWELL SABRE 75A

Country of Origin: USA.

Type: Light business executive transport.

Power Plant: Two 4,315 lb (1 961 kg) General Electric CF700-2D-2 turbofans.

Performance: Max. cruise (at 21,370 lb/9 693 kg), 563 mph (906 km/h); long-range cruise, 488 mph (785 km/h); range (six passengers and 45 min reserves), 1,894 mls (3 048 km), (10 passengers and 45 min reserves), 1,695 mls (2 730 km); initial climb (at 23,000 lb/10 433 kg), 4,500 ft/min (22,86 m/sec).

Weights: Empty equipped, 13,350 lb (6 056 kg); max. take-off, 23,000 lb (10 433 kg).

Accommodation: Normal flight crew of two and various arrangements for six to 10 passengers.

Status: First prototype Sabre 75A flown initially on October 18, 1972, with second following on December 1, 1972. First customer delivery February 1974, with deliveries averaging 1·5 per month through remainder of year.

Notes: The Sabre 75A is a variant of the Sabre 75 (see 1972 edition) which it replaces and from which it differs primarily in having turbofans in place of JT12A-8 turbojets. The Sabre 75A employs the same wings as those of the Sabre Commander 40A and the Sabreliner Series 60 (see 1968 edition) but has an entirely new fuselage of deeper section. Eleven Sabre 75As were ordered for the US Federal Aviation Administration for navaid checking.

ROCKWELL SABRE 75A

Dimensions: Span, 44 ft 6 in (13,56 m); length, 47 ft 2 in (14,37 m); height, 17 ft 3 in (5,26 m); wing area, 342·05 sq ft (31,78 m²).

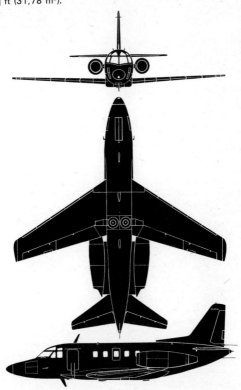

ROCKWELL TURBO COMMANDER 690A

Country of Origin: USA.

Type: Light business executive transport.

Power Plant: Two 700 shp Garrett AiResearch TPE 331-5-251 turboprops.

Performance: Max. speed, 328 mph (528 km/h); max. cruise, 322 mph (518 km/h) at 17,500 ft (5 334 m), 321 mph (516 km/h) at 20,000 ft (6 096 m); max. range (with 45 min reserves), 1,693 mls (2 724 km) at 31,000 ft (9 450 m); initial climb, 2,849 ft/min (14,5 m/sec); service ceiling, 33,000 ft (10 058 m).

Weights: Empty, 6,126 lb (2 779 kg); max. take-off, 10,250 lb (4 649 kg).

Accommodation: Two seats side-by-side on flight deck and various alternative arrangements for five–nine passengers in the main cabin.

Status: The prototype Commander 690 was flown on March 3, 1969, and was certificated on July 19, 1971. The Commander 690 was supplanted by the improved Commander 690A late 1973, and monthly customer deliveries averaged 7–8 aircraft during 1974.

Notes: The Commander 690A is a progressive improvement of the original Aero Commander (Model 680T) Turbo Commander, and is manufactured in parallel with the Commander 685 which uses an essentially similar airframe but is powered by 435 hp Continental GTSIO-520F six-cylinder horizontally-opposed piston engines (see 1973 edition). The Turbo Commander 690 holds a world class record with an average speed of 380 mph (611,5 km/h) over a measured 500-km (310·69-mile) course.

ROCKWELL TURBO COMMANDER 690A

Dimension: Span, 46 ft $6\frac{2}{3}$ in (14,23 m); length, 44 ft $4\frac{1}{4}$ in (13,55 m); height, 14 ft $11\frac{1}{3}$ in (4,56 m); wing area, 266 sq ft (24,70 m²).

173

SAAB SUPPORTER

Country of Origin: Sweden.

Type: Two-seat primary trainer, forward air control and light close support aircraft.

Power Plant: One 200 hp Avco Lycoming IO-360-A1B6 four-cylinder horizontally-opposed engine.

Performance: Max. speed (at 1,984 lb/900 kg), 155 mph (250 km/h) at sea level, (at 2,425 lb/1 100 kg), 153 mph (246 km/h); cruise at 75% power (at 1,984 lb/900 kg), 138 mph (222 km/h) at sea level; range (clean aircraft with 10% reserves), 580 mls (933 km) at 130 mph (209 km/h) at sea level; initial climb (at 2,204 lb/1 000 kg), 1,082 ft/min (5,5 m/sec).

Weights: Empty, 1,415 lb (642 kg); max. take-off, 2,425 lb (1 100 kg).

Armament (Close support role) Six underwing hardpoints of which two inboard stressed for 330-lb (150-kg) loads and remainder for 220-lb (100-kg) loads. Max. weight of ordnance (including pylons) is 661 lb (300 kg), typical loads including six Bofors anti-tank missiles, 18 75-mm Bofors rockets, two 7,62-mm gun pods, or four Abel pods each with seven 68-mm rockets.

Status: Prototype flown (as MFI 15) on July 11, 1969, with first of 12 pre-production (Safari/Supporter) aircraft following on April 9, 1973. Initial production batch of 65 begun July 1974 with deliveries scheduled from February 1975.

Notes: Safari (originally MFI 15) is civil equivalent of Supporter (originally MFI 17), 45 of the latter having been ordered by Pakistan.

SAAB SUPPORTER

Dimensions: Span, 29 ft 0½ in (8,85 m); length, 22 ft 11½ in (7,00 m); height, 8 ft 6¼ in (2,60 m); wing area, 128·09 sq ft (11,90 m²).

SAAB (JA) 37 VIGGEN

Country of Origin: Sweden.
Type: Single-seat all-weather interceptor fighter with secondary strike capability.
Power Plant: One 28,085 lb (12 740 kg) reheat Volvo Flygmotor RM 8B turbofan.
Performance: (Estimated) Max. speed (without external stores), 1,320 mph (2 125 km/h) above 36,090 ft (11 000 m) or Mach 2·0, 875 mph (1 410 km/h) at 1,000 ft (305 m) or Mach 1·15; operational radius (typical intercept armament), 700+ mls (1 126+ km); initial climb, 20,000 ft/min (101,6 m/sec); time to 36,090 ft (11 000 m), 2 min.
Weights: Approx. normal max. take-off, 35,274 lb (16 000 kg).
Armament: One semi-externally mounted 30-mm Oerlikon KCA cannon plus mix of infra-red and radar homing AAMs.
Status: First of six AJ 37 prototypes flown February 8, 1967 and first production AJ 37 flown February 23, 1971; two-seat SK 37 prototype flown July 2, 1970, with first production SK 37 delivery following in June 1972; first SF 37 flown May 21, 1973, and first of four JA 37 prototypes (modified from AJ 37 airframes) flown June 1974 and second (with RM 8B engine) flown September 27, 1974. Pre-production JA 37 scheduled to fly mid-1975. Orders placed by beginning of 1975 for 210 Viggens, including 30 JA 37s.
Notes: JA 37 is optimised for intercept role with uprated engine, cannon armament and L. M. Ericsson X-Band Pulse Doppler radar. The second JA 37 prototype is illustrated above.

SAAB (JA) 37 VIGGEN

Dimensions: Span, 34 ft 9¼ in (10,60 m); length (excluding probe), 50 ft 8¼ in (15,45 m); height, 18 ft 4½ in (5,60 m); wing area (including foreplanes), 567·22 sq ft (52,70 m²).

SAUNDERS ST-27B

Country of Origin: Canada.
Type: Third-level airliner.
Power Plant: Two 940 ehp UACL PT6A-34 turboprops.
Performance: Max. cruise, 233 mph (375 km/h) at 10,000 ft (3 048 m); econ. cruise, 210 mph (338 km/h) at 7,000 ft (2 135 m); range (with max. payload and reserves for 45 min hold), 230 mls (370 km) at 10,000 ft (3 048 m); max. range (no reserves), 1,185 mls (1 908 km); service ceiling, 25,000 ft (7 620 m).
Weights: Typical empty, 8,824 lb (4 002 kg); max. take-off, 14,500 lb (6 576 kg).
Accommodation: Flight crew of two with standard arrangement for 22 passengers in individual seats.
Status: The original ST-27 was a turboprop-powered remanufactured and "stretched" version of the D.H.114 Heron, the prototype flying on May 28, 1969. A further 12 remanufactured aircraft were delivered, one being modified as the ST-27A to the proposed ST-27B standard and flying on July 17, 1974. The ST-27B is, unlike its predecessors, of wholly original construction; an initial production batch of 15 is in hand and deliveries are scheduled for mid-1975 with a planned production rate of three per month by 1977.
Notes: The ST-27B differs from the original ST-27 primarily in having a redesigned flight deck windscreen, metal-skinned flying control surfaces, an enlarged dorsal fin and increased fuel capacity, and embodies a complete structure and systems redesign.

SAUNDERS ST-27B

Dimensions: Span, 71 ft 6 in (21,79 m); length, 58 ft 10 in (17,93 m); height, 15 ft 7 in (4,75 m); wing area, 499 sq ft (46,36 m²).

SCOTTISH AVIATION BULLDOG 200

Country of Origin: United Kingdom.

Type: Four-seat multi-purpose light military aircraft.

Power Plant: One 200 hp Avco Lycoming IO-360-A1B6 four-cylinder horizontally-opposed engine.

Performance: (Estimated) Max. speed, 173 mph (278 km/h) at sea level; cruise at 75% power, 162 mph (261 km/h) at 4,000 ft (1 220 m); max. fuel range (at 55% power), 680 mls (1 094 km); max. endurance, 5 hrs; initial climb, 1,160 ft/min (5,9 m/sec); service ceiling, 18,500 ft (5 639 m).

Weights: Typical empty operational, 1,810 lb (820 kg); max. aerobatic, 2,293 lb (1 040 kg); max. take-off, 2,601 lb (1 180 kg).

Armament: (Light strike role and weapons training) Four wing hardpoints with combined maximum capacity of 640 lb (290 kg) of ordnance.

Status: Prototype scheduled to fly during second half of 1975 with production deliveries commencing in 1976.

Notes: The Bulldog 200 is a progressive development of the fixed-gear Bulldog 120 (see 1974 edition) which is intended to complement but not replace the earlier model. Suitable for use as a weapons trainer, for light strike duties, for basic and aerobatic training, for liaison and tactical reconnaissance, and other military roles, the Bulldog 200 has a fully retractable undercarriage, provision for a fourth seat in the cockpit, a lengthened and cleaner engine cowling, a repositioned fire-wall and a "plug" type canopy of revised contour. First 98 production Bulldogs were of the Series 100 version, this being succeeded by the Series 120 embodying minor improvements and currently in production.

SCOTTISH AVIATION BULLDOG 200

Dimensions: Span, 33 ft 0 in (10,06 m); length, 22 ft 3 in (7,08 m); height, 7 ft 5¾ in (2,28 m); wing area, 129·4 sq ft (12,02 m²).

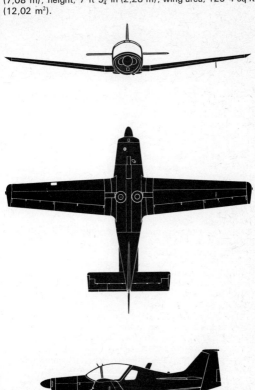

SCOTTISH AVIATION JETSTREAM 201

Country of Origin: United Kingdom.
Type: Light business executive and utility transport.
Power Plant: Two 940 eshp Turboméca Astazou XVI turbo-props.
Performance: Max. cruise, 278 mph (448 km/h) at 12,000 ft (3 660 m), 254 mph (409 km/h) at 22,000 ft (6 705 m); range with max. fuel and 5% reserves plus 45 min hold, 1,382 mls (2 224 km); initial climb, 2,500 ft/min (12,7 m/sec); service ceiling, 26,000 ft (7 928 m).
Weights: Empty equipped (executive), 9,286 lb (4 212 kg); max. take-off, 12,550 lb (5 692 kg).
Accommodation: Normal flight crew of two and 12 passengers in executive layout with alternative 12–18 passenger commuter arrangements.
Status: Development initiated by Handley Page as the Jetstream 2, and flight testing resumed by Jetstream Aircraft Limited as the Jetstream Series 200 in December 1970. Production subsequently taken over by Scottish Aviation. Delivery of 26 pilot-training aircraft to the RAF commenced June 1973 as Jetstream T. Mk. 1, and was continuing at the beginning of 1975.
Notes: The initial Handley Page-built version was the Jetstream 1 with Astazou XIV engines, 36 production examples of which were completed. Development of the Astazou XVI-powered Jetstream 2 was initiated by Handley Page with the re-engined first pre-production aircraft. All development is now being undertaken by Scottish Aviation and initial assessments have been made for a variant with a higher gross weight and alternative engines for possible delivery in 1976.

SCOTTISH AVIATION JETSTREAM 201

Dimensions: Span, 52 ft 0 in (15,85 m); length, 47 ft 1½ in (14,37 m); height, 17 ft 5½ in (5,32 m); wing area, 270 sq ft (25,08 m²).

SEPECAT JAGUAR G.R. MK. 1

Countries of Origin: France and United Kingdom.

Type: Single-seat tactical strike fighter.

Power Plant: Two 4,620 lb (2 100 kg) dry and 7,140 lb (3 240 kg) reheat Rolls-Royce Turboméca RT.172 Adour 102 turbofans.

Performance: (At typical weight) Max. speed, 820 mph (1 320 km/h) or Mach 1·1 at 1,000 ft (305 m), 1,057 mph (1 700 km/h) or Mach 1·6 at 32,810 ft (10 000 m); cruise with max. ordnance, 430 mph (690 km/h) or Mach 0·65 at 39,370 ft (12 000 m); range with external fuel for lo-lo-lo mission profile, 450 mls (724 km), for hi-lo-hi mission profile, 710 mls (1 142 km); ferry range, 2,270 mls (3 650 km).

Weights: Normal take-off, 23,000 lb (10 430 kg); max. take-off, 32,600 lb (14 790 kg).

Armament: Two 30-mm Aden cannon and up to 10,000 lb (4 536 kg) ordnance on five external hardpoints.

Status: First of eight prototypes flown September 8, 1968. First production Jaguar E for France flown November 2, 1971, with first Jaguar A following April 20, 1972. First production Jaguar S for UK flown October 11, 1972. By the beginning of 1975, France had ordered 170 Jaguars and the UK had ordered 202.

Notes: Both France and UK have a requirement for approximately 200 Jaguars, French versions being the single-seat A (*Appui Tactique*) and two-seat E (*École de Combat*), and British versions being the single-seat S (G.R. Mk. 1) and the two-seat B (T Mk. 2). The G.R. Mk. 1 differs from the Jaguar A in having a nose-mounted laser rangefinder and tail-mounted avionics pack. The export Jaguar International with uprated Adour 804 engines has been ordered by Oman (12) and Ecuador (12).

SEPECAT JAGUAR G.R. MK. 1

Dimensions: Span, 28 ft 6 in (8,69 m); length, 50 ft 11 in (15,52 m); height, 16 ft 0½ in (4,89 m); wing area, 260·3 sq ft (24,18 m²).

SHIN MEIWA US-1

Country of Origin: Japan.

Type: Amphibious search and rescue flying boat.

Power Plant: Four 3,060 ehp Ishikawajima-Harima-built General Electric T64-IHI-10 turboprops.

Performance: Max. speed, 311 mph (500 km/h) at 9,840 ft (3 000 m); high-speed cruise, 265 mph (426 km/h) at 9,840 ft (3 000 m); long-range cruise (two engines), 202 mph (325 km/h) at 8,200 ft (2 500 m); loiter speed, 161 mph (259 km/h) at 1,000 ft (305 m); search endurance, 6 hrs at 690-mile (1 110 km) range; max. search and rescue range, 3,145 mls (5 060 km); initial climb, 2,360 ft/min (12,0 m/sec); service ceiling, 28,000 ft (8 535 m).

Weights: Empty equipped, 52,690 lb (23 900 kg); max. take-off, 99,208 lb (45 000 kg).

Accommodation: Crew of eight comprising pilot, co-pilot, flight engineer, radar operator, navigator, radio operator, observer and rescue man. Up to five medical attendants and 36 stretcher casualties.

Status: First of three US-1s ordered by the Japanese Maritime Self-Defence Force flown October 16, 1974, with delivery scheduled for March 1975, delivery of second and third aircraft planned for June and December 1975 respectively.

Notes: The US-1 (alias SS-2A) is an amphibious rescue derivative of the SS-2 maritime patrol flying boat (see 1974 edition). Featuring a retractable undercarriage, the main twinwheel members of which retract into bulged housings, the US-1 has a 1,400 ehp General Electric T58-10 turboshaft driving a boundary-layer control compressor for the flaps, elevators and rudder.

186

SHIN MEIWA US-1

Dimensions: Span, 107 ft 6½ in (32,78 m); length, 109 ft 11 in (33,50 m); height, 32 ft 3 in (9,83 m); wing area, 1,453·13 sq ft (135,00 m²).

SHORT SKYVAN SERIES 3M

Country of Origin: United Kingdom.
Type: Light military utility transport.
Power Plant: Two 715 shp Garrett AiResearch TPE 331-201 turboprops.
Performance: Max. cruise, 201 mph (323 km/h) at 10,000 ft (3 050 m); econ. cruise, 173 mph (278 km/h) at 10,000 ft (3 050 m); range with max. fuel and 45 min reserves, 660 mls (1 062 km), with 5,000-lb (2 268-kg) payload and same reserves, 166 mls (267 km); initial climb, 1,520 ft/min (7,6 m/sec); service ceiling, 21,000 ft (6 400 m).
Weights: Basic operational, 7,400 lb (3 356 kg); max. take-off, 14,500 lb (6 577 kg).
Accommodation: Flight crew of one or two, and up to 22 fully-equipped troops, 16 paratroops and a despatcher, or 12 casualty stretchers and two medical attendants.
Status: Series 3M prototype flown in 1970. Interspersed on assembly line with civil Series 3, and combined production running at two per month at beginning of 1975 with more than 100 delivered. Orders have included 16 for the Sultan of Oman's Air Force, five for Argentine Navy, two for Nepalese Army, six for the Singapore Air Defence Command, six for the Ghana Air Force, two for the North Yemeni air arm, and one for the Ecuador Army.
Notes: The Series 3M (illustrated opposite with nose weather radar) is the military equivalent of the civil Series 3A.

SHORT SKYVAN SERIES 3M

Dimensions: Span, 64 ft 11 in (19,79 m); length, 40 ft 1 in (12,21 m), with radome, 41 ft 4 in (12,60 m); height, 15 ft 1 in (4,60 m); wing area, 373 sq ft (34,65 m²).

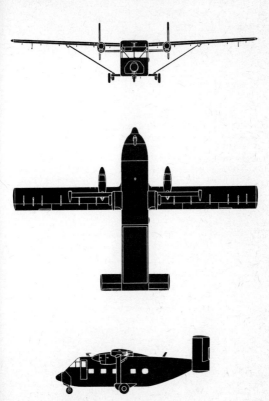

SHORT SD3-30

Country of Origin: United Kingdom.

Type: Third-level airliner.

Power Plant: Two 1,120 shp UACL PT6A-45 turboprops.

Performance: High speed cruise, 226 mph (363 km/h) at 5,000 ft (1 525 m), 228 mph (367 km/h) at 10,000 ft (3 050 m); long-range cruise, 180 mph (289 km/h) at 5,000 ft (1 525 m), 184 mph (296 km/h) at 10,000 ft (3 050 m); range (30 passengers and reserves for 45 min hold and 100-ml/160-km diversion), 276 mls (444 km) at long-range cruise, (with 20 passengers), 870 mls (1 400 km); initial climb, 1,200 ft/min (6,10 m/sec).

Weights: Basic empty, 11,500 lb (5 215 kg); operational empty (airliner), 13,890 lb (6 300 kg); max. take-off, 21,700 lb (9 840 kg).

Accommodation: Standard flight crew of two and 30 passengers in 10 rows three abreast. Total of 1,000 lb (455 kg) baggage may be accommodated in aft and nose compartments.

Status: Engineering prototype flown August 22, 1974, to be followed by production prototype with first customer deliveries (to Command Airways) early 1976. Anticipated production of three—four per month by end of 1976.

Notes: Owing much to the Skyvan (see pages 188–89), the SD3-30 has been optimised for commuter and regional air services. A large forward cargo door capable of accepting D-size containers facilitates use of the aircraft in mixed passenger/cargo configuration when a 7,500-lb (3 402-kg) payload may be carried. A military variant, the SD3-M capable of accommodating 34 troops, is projected with optional full-width rear-loading door.

SHORT SD3-30

Dimensions: Span, 74 ft 9 in (22,78 m); length, 58 ft 0½ in (17,69 m); height, 15 ft 8 in (4,78 m); wing area, 453 sq ft (42,10 m²).

SIAI-MARCHETTI SM.1019A

Country of Origin: Italy.
Type: Battlefield surveillance and forward air control aircraft.
Power Plant: One 317 shp Allison 250-B15G turboprop.
Performance: Max. speed (at 2,293 lb/1 040 kg), 182 mph (293 km/h) at sea level; max. cruise, 155 mph (250 km/h) at 6,000 ft (1 830 m); econ. cruise, 135 mph (217 km/h) at 10,000 ft (3 050 m); range with max. fuel and 10 min reserves, 765 mls (1 230 km), with 500-lb (227-kg) external stores on wing stations and same reserves, 320 mls (515 km); initial climb, 1,625 ft (8,25 m/sec).
Weights: Empty equipped, 1,499 lb (680 kg); max. take-off, 2,800 lb (1 270 kg).
Armament: Two stores stations under wings capable of carrying minigun pods, rockets, etc., up to a maximum external load of 500 lb (227 kg).
Status: First of two prototypes flown May 24, 1969 and second on February 18, 1971. A production line for 100 aircraft has been laid down and the first production aircraft were expected to fly late 1974.
Notes: The SM.1019 is based upon the Cessna O-1 Bird Dog but possesses an extensively modified airframe to meet latest operational requirements, redesigned tail surfaces, and a turboprop in place of the O-1's piston engine. The second prototype, the SM.1019A, has a second door for the observer and duplicated instrument panel. The SM.1019 competed with the AM.3C (see 1974 edition) for a production order for the Italian Army, and was selected as the winning contender.

192

SIAI-MARCHETTI SM.1019A

Dimensions: Span, 36 ft 0 in (10,97 m); length, 27 ft 10$\frac{2}{3}$ in (8,52 m); height, 7 ft 9$\frac{3}{4}$ in (2,38 m); wing area, 173·94 sq ft (16,16 m²).

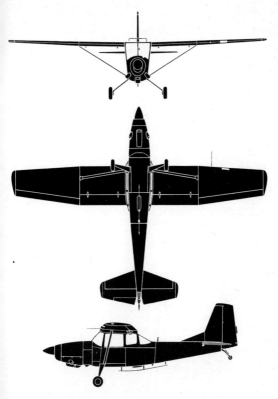

SIAI-MARCHETTI SF.260W WARRIOR

Country of Origin: Italy.

Type: Side-by-side two-seat light tactical and training aircraft.

Power Plant: One 260 hp Avco Lycoming O-540-E4A5 six-cylinder horizontally-opposed engine.

Performance: (Without external stores) Max. speed, 230 mph (370 km/h) at sea level; max. cruise, 214 mph (345 km/h) at 10,000 ft (3 050 m); econ. cruise, 203 mph (327 km/h) at 10,000 ft (3 050 m); max. range, 1,275 mls (2 050 km); initial climb, 1,770 ft/min (10 m/sec).

Weights: Empty equipped, 1,764 lb (800 kg); max. take-off, 2,879–2998 lb (1 306–1 360 kg).

Armament: Stores pylons for maximum of 661 lb (300 kg) of ordnance. Typical ordnance loads comprise two Matra gun pods each containing two 7,62-mm MAC AAF1 machine guns, two Alkan 20AP cartridge throwers, two Simpres AL18-50 pods each containing 18 2-in (5,0-cm) rockets or AL9-70 pods each containing nine 2·75-in (6,98-cm) rockets, or two 110-lb (50-kg) or 264·5-lb (120-kg) bombs.

Status: The prototype SF.260W was flown for the first time in May 1972. Production of SF.260 and SF.260W continuing at beginning of 1975.

Notes: The Warrior is an armed version of the SF.260MX trainer, the generic designation of the export military version of the SF.260 cabin monoplane of which deliveries commenced in 1970. The SF.260MX has been supplied to Belgium (30), Zaïre (12), Zambia (8), Singapore (16), Philippines (48 including 16 SF.260Ws), Thailand (12), Tunisia (12 SF.260Ws), Morocco (2) and Dubai (1).

SIAI-MARCHETTI SF.260W WARRIOR

Dimensions: Span, 26 ft 11¾ in (8,25 m); length, 23 ft 0 in (7,02 m); height, 8 ft 6 in (2,60 m); wing area, 108·5 sq ft (10,1 m²).

SUKHOI SU-15 (FLAGON-A)

Country of Origin: USSR.

Type: Single-seat all-weather interceptor fighter.

Power Plant: Two 17,195 lb (7 800 kg) dry and 24,700 lb (11 200 kg) reheat Lyulka AL-21F turbojets.

Performance: (Estimated) Max. speed without external stores, 1,650 mph (2 655 km/h) or Mach 2·5 at 39,370 ft (12 000 m), 910 mph (1 465 km/h) or Mach 1·2 at 1,000 ft (305 m), with AAMs on wing stations and twin drop tanks on fuselage stations, 1,120 mph (1 800 km/h) or Mach 1·7 at 39,370 ft (12 000 m); range at subsonic cruise with max. external fuel, 1,500 mls (2 415 km).

Weights: (Estimated) Normal take-off, 35,000–40,000 lb (15 875–18 145 kg).

Armament: Basic armament for intercept mission reportedly comprises two AAMs of Advanced Anab type on wing stations.

Status: The Su-15 is believed to have flown in prototype form during 1964–65 with production deliveries commencing 1969, and some 400 were alleged by US official sources to be in service with the Soviet Air Forces by mid-1971 when production was believed to be some 15 aircraft monthly.

Notes: Apparently optimised for the intercept role as a successor to the Su-11 (see 1973 edition), the Su-15 is in large-scale service with the Soviet Air Forces. A STOL version with three direct lift engines in the centre fuselage, the Flagon-B, was apparently purely a technology development aircraft, but the extended wings with compound sweep featured by this model is utilised by two service versions, the Flagon-D and -E. A two-seat conversion training version of the Flagon-A is known as the Flagon-C.

SUKHOI SU-15 (FLAGON-A)

Dimensions: (Estimated) Span, 31 ft 3 in (9,50 m); length, 70 ft 6 in (21,50 m); height, 16 ft 6 in (5,00 m).

SUKHOI SU-20

Country of Origin: USSR.

Type: Single-seat strike fighter.

Power Plant: One 17,195 lb (7 800 kg) dry and 24,700 lb (11 200 kg) reheat Lyulka AL-21F-3 turbojet.

Performance: Max. speed (clean), 808 mph (1 300 km/h) or Mach 1·06 at sea level, 1,430 mph (2 300 km/h) at 39,370 ft (12 000 m) or Mach 2·17; combat radius (lo-lo-lo mission profile), 260 mls (420 km), (hi-lo-hi mission profile), 373 mls (600 km); range (with 2,205-lb/1 000-kg weapon load and auxiliary fuel), 1,415 mls (2 280 km); service ceiling, 57,415 ft (17 500 m).

Weights: Max. take-off, 39,022 lb (17 700 kg).

Armament: Two 30-mm NR-30 cannon with 70 rpg and (for short-range missions) a max. external ordnance load of 7,716 lb (3 500 kg). Typical external stores include UV-16-57 or UV-32-57 rocket pods containing 16 and 32 55-mm S-5 rockets respectively, 240-mm S-24 rockets, or 550-lb (250-kg) or 1,100-lb (500-kg) bombs.

Status: The Su-20 entered service with the Soviet Air Forces in 1972, and is currently being exported to Warsaw Pact countries, entering service with the Polish Air Force during the course of 1974.

Notes: The Su-20 is a variable-geometry strike fighter derivative of the Su-7 (see 1973 edition), a variable-geometry technology demonstration version of which was first seen at Domodedovo in July 1967. The Su-20 retains much of the structure of the earlier Su-7 and features the deep dorsal spine first introduced on the tandem two-seat Su-7U(Moujik), this containing fuel.

SUKHOI SU-20

Estimated Dimensions: Span (max.), 45 ft 0 in (13,70 m), (min.), 32 ft 6 in (9,90 m); length (including probe), 57 ft 0 in (17,37 m); height, 15 ft 5 in (4,70 m).

TUPOLEV (BACKFIRE)

Country of Origin: USSR.

Type: Strategic bomber.

Power Plant: Two (approx.) 40,000 lb (18 144 kg) reheat turbofans.

Performance: (Estimated) Max. speed (clean), 975 mph (1 570 km/h) at 3,280 ft (1 000 m) or Mach 1·3, (with semi-internally mounted ASM-6 stand-off missile), 1,450–1,650 mph (2 330–2 655 km/h) above 36,090 ft (11 000 m) or Mach 2·2 to 2·5; max. unrefuelled range, 4,500 mls (7 240 km) plus at 39,370 ft (12 000 m); operational ceiling, 50,000 ft (15 240 m) plus.

Weights: Approx. normal take-off, 275,000 lb (124 740 kg).

Armament: Primary attack armament comprises one ASM-6 stand-off missile with range of approx. 460 mls (740 km).

Status: First reported in prototype form in 1969, with initial service introduction commencing in 1973.

Notes: The variable-geometry strategic bomber assigned the reporting name "Backfire" and believed to match the performance of the Rockwell B-1 (see pages 164–5) in key areas, is apparently serving with the Soviet Air Forces in two versions, that illustrated (Backfire-A) and one with a modified wing configuration and a revised undercarriage arrangement, the main bogies being transferred from wing trailing-edge fairings to the fuselage (Backfire-B).

TUPOLEV (BACKFIRE)

Dimensions: No details available for publication.

TUPOLEV (MOSS)

Country of Origin: USSR.

Type: Airborne warning and control system aircraft.

Power Plant: Four 14,795 ehp Kuznetsov NK-12MV turbo-props.

Performance: (Estimated) Max. continuous cruise, 460 mph (740 km/h) at 25,000 ft (7 620 m); max. unrefuelled range, 4,000+ mls (6 440+ km); service ceiling, 39,000 ft (11 890 m).

Weights: (Estimated) Normal max. take-off, 360,000 lb (163 290 kg).

Accommodation: Operational complement is likely to comprise a flight crew of four and a systems operation crew of about 10–12, plus provision for relief and maintenance crews.

Status: The AWACS aircraft assigned the reporting name *Moss* by the Air Standards Co-ordinating Committee became known to Western intelligence agencies in the mid 'sixties, and first appeared in service in 1970.

Notes: Essentially an adaptation of the Tu-114 commercial transport, and apparently retaining the wings, tail surfaces, power plant and undercarriage of the earlier aircraft, the Tupolev AWACS type is primarily intended to locate low-flying intruders and to vector interceptors towards them. The dominating feature of the aircraft is its pylon-mounted saucer-shaped early-warning scanner housing of approximately 37·5 ft (12,00 m) diameter. Flight refuelling capability is provided, the fuel line being carried from the probe along the starboard side of the fuselage.

TUPOLEV (MOSS)

Dimensions: Span, 168 ft 0 in (51,20 m); approx. length, 188 ft 0 in (57,30 m); height, 51 ft 0 in (15,50 m); wing area, 3,349 sq ft (311,1 m²).

TUPOLEV TU-22 (BLINDER)

Country of Origin: USSR.

Type: Long-range medium bomber and strike-reconnaissance aircraft.

Power Plant: Two (approx.) 27,000 lb (12 250 kg) reheat turbojets.

Performance: (Estimated) Max. speed without external stores, 990 mph (1 590 km/h) or Mach 1·5 at 39,370 ft (12 000 m), 720 mph (1 160 km/h) or Mach 0·95 at 1,000 ft (305 m); normal cruise, 595 mph (960 km/h) or Mach 0·9 at 39,370 ft (12 000 m); tactical radius on standard fuel for high-altitude mission, 700 mls (1 125 km); service ceiling, 60,000 ft (18 290 m).

Weights: (Estimated) Max. take-off, 185,000 lb (84 000 kg).

Armament: Free-falling weapons housed internally or (Blinder-B) semi-recessed Kitchen ASM. Remotely-controlled 23-mm cannon in tail barbette.

Status: Believed to have attained operational status with the Soviet Air Forces in 1965. Production continuing into 1975.

Notes: The Tu-22 is the successor to the subsonic Tu-16 in Soviet medium-bomber formations and with shore-based maritime strike elements of the Soviet Naval Air Arm (Blinder C). The basic version (illustrated above) is dubbed Blinder-A by NATO, the missile-carrying Blinder-B being illustrated on the opposite page. A training version, the Blinder-D, features a raised second cockpit for the instructor. Recent production models of the Tu-22 display a number of modifications, including an extended flight refuelling probe and enlarged engine air intakes, nacelles and exhaust orifices. During the course of 1974, a long-range heavy interceptor version of the Tu-22 was being phased in as a successor to the Tu-28P.

TUPOLEV TU-22 (BLINDER)

Dimensions: (Estimated) Span, 91 ft 0 in (27,74 m); length, 133 ft 0 in (40,50 m); height, 17 ft 0 in (5,18 m); wing area, 2,030 sq ft (188,59 m²).

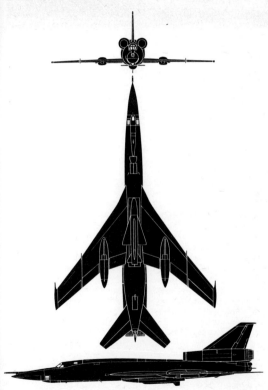

TUPOLEV TU-134A (CRUSTY)

Country of Origin: USSR.

Type: Short- to medium-range commercial transport.

Power Plant: Two 14,990 lb (6 800 kg) Soloviev D-30-2 Turbofans.

Performance: Max. cruise, 528 mph (850 km/h) at 32,810 ft (10 000 m); long-range cruise, 466 mph (750 km/h) at 32,810 ft (10 000 m); max. range at long-range cruise with 1 hr reserves and 18,108-lb (8 215-kg) payload, 1,243 mls (2 000 km), with 8,818-lb (4 000-kg) payload, 2,175 mls (3 500 km).

Weights: Operational empty, 63,934 lb (29 000 kg); max. take-off, 103,617 lb (47 000 kg).

Accommodation: Basic flight crew of three and maximum of 80 passengers in four-abreast all-tourist class configuration.

Status: Prototype Tu-134A flown in 1968 and first production deliveries (to *Aeroflot*) mid-1970. Series production continuing at Kharkov at the beginning of 1975.

Notes: The Tu-134A differs from the original Tu-134, which entered *Aeroflot* service in 1966, in having an additional 6 ft 10⅜ in (2,10 m) section inserted in the fuselage immediately forward of the wing to permit two additional rows of passenger seats, and introduces engine thrust reversers. Maximum take-off weight has been increased by 5,512 lb (2 500 kg), maximum payload being raised by 1,025 lb (465 kg), an APU is provided, and radio and navigational equipment have been revised. Route proving trials with the Tu-134A were completed by *Aeroflot* late in 1970, and this airliner was introduced on international routes early in 1971. The shorter-fuselage Tu-134 serves with Aeroflot, CSA, Interflug, LOT, Malev, Bulair, Balkan-Bulgarian and Aviogenex.

TUPOLEV TU-134A (CRUSTY)

Dimensions: Span, 95 ft 2 in (29,00 m); length, 111 ft 0½ in (36,40 m); height, 29 ft 7 in (9,02 m); wing area, 1,370·3 sq ft (127,3 m²).

TUPOLEV TU-144 (CHARGER)

Country of Origin: USSR.
Type: Long-range supersonic commercial transport.
Power Plant: Four 33,100 lb (15 000 kg) dry and 44,000 lb (20 000 kg) reheat Kuznetsov NK-144 turbofans.
Performance: Max. cruise, 1,550 mph (2 500 km/h) or Mach 2·3 at altitudes up to 59,000 ft (18 000 m); subsonic cruise, 614 mph (988 km/h) or Mach 0·93 at 37,730 ft (11 500 m); range (with full payload), 4,000 mls (6 440 km); cruising altitude, 52,500 ft (16 460 m) to 59,000 ft (18 000 m).
Weights: Typical operational empty, 187,395 lb (85 000 kg); max. take-off, 396,830 lb (180 000 kg).
Accommodation: Basic flight crew of three and maximum of up to 140 passengers in single-class arrangement with three-plus-two and two-plus-two seating.
Status: First pre-production aircraft (representative of the production configuration) flown September 1971, and six aircraft of production standard were expected to have flown by mid-1974 when a production rate of one every three weeks was scheduled against an anticipated Aeroflot requirement for approximately 75 aircraft. Initial passenger services are expected to be flown within the Soviet Union late 1975.
Notes: The production-standard Tu-144 described and illustrated on these pages shares little more than a generally similar configuration with the prototype to which this designation was first applied and which flew for the first time on December 31, 1968. The current model has been lengthened by 20 ft 8 in (6,30 m) and the compound delta wing is of 3 ft 9 in (1,15 m) greater span than the ogee wing of the original aircraft; the uprated engines are housed by relocated nacelles, and retractable noseplanes have been added.

TUPOLEV TU-144 (CHARGER)

Dimensions: Span, 94 ft 6 in (28,80 m); length, 215 ft 6½ in (65,70 m); height, 42 ft 3 in (12,85 m); wing area, 4,720 sq ft (438 m²).

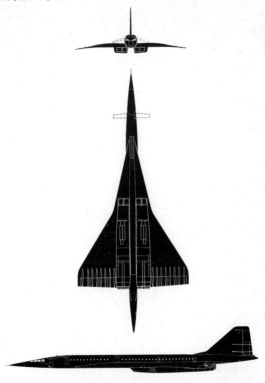

TUPOLEV TU-154 (CARELESS)

Country of Origin: USSR.

Type: Medium- to long-range commercial transport.

Power Plant: Three 20,950 lb (9 500 kg) Kuznetsov NK-8-2 turbofans.

Performance: Max. cruise, 605 mph (975 km/h) at 31,170 ft (9 500 m); long-range cruise, 528 mph (850 km/h) at 37,730 ft (11 500 m); range with standard fuel and reserves of 1 hr plus 6% and max. payload, 2,150 mls (3 460 km) at 560 mph (900 km/h), 2,360 mls (3 800 km) at 528 mph (850 km/h).

Weights: Operational empty, 95,900 lb (43 500 kg); normal take-off, 185,188 lb (84 000 kg); max. take-off, 198,416 lb (90 000 kg).

Accommodation: Basic flight crew of three–four, and alternative arrangements for 158 or 150 economy-class passengers, 150, 146 or 136 tourist-class passengers, or 24 first-class and 104 tourist-class passengers.

Status: First prototype flown October 4, 1968, with first delivery of a production aircraft (to *Aeroflot*) following August 1970, route proving commencing August 1971.

Notes: The Tu-154 entered service on *Aeroflot* routes early 1972, and is intended as a successor to the Tu-104, Il-18 and An-10 on medium- to long-range routes. It can operate from airfields with category B surfaces, including packed earth and gravel. Operators include Balkan-Bulgarian, and Malev of Hungary. Egyptair operated the Tu-154 briefly during 1974. A growth version, referred to as the Tu-154M and reportedly flown in March 1974, is currently under development. This model incorporates additional fuselage sections which will enable 220–240 passengers to be carried, and 25,350 lb (11 500 kg) D-30KU engines.

TUPOLEV TU-154 (CARELESS)

Dimensions: Span, 123 ft 2½ in (37,55 m); length, 157 ft 1¾ in (47,90 m); height, 37 ft 4¾ in (11,40 m); wing area, 2,168·92 sq ft (201,45 m²).

VFW-FOKKER VFW 614

Country of Origin: Federal Germany.

Type: Short-range commercial transport.

Power Plant: Two 7,510 (3 410 kg) Rolls-Royce/SNECMA M45H turbofans.

Performance: Max. cruise, 457 mph (735 km/h) at 21,000 ft (6 400 m); long-range cruise, 367 mph (591 km/h) at 25,000 ft (7 620 m); range with max. fuel, 1,841 mls (2 963 km), with max. payload, 978 mls (1 574 km); initial climb rate, 3,410 ft/min (17,3 m/sec).

Weights: Operational empty, 27,557 lb (12 500 kg); max. take-off, 44,200 lb (20 050 kg).

Accommodation: Basic flight crew of two and alternative passenger configurations for 36, 40 or 44 seats in four-abreast rows.

Status: First of three prototypes commenced its flight test programme on June 14, 1971, with second and third following on August 19 and October 10, 1972. First production aircraft scheduled for delivery (to Cimber Air of Denmark) mid-1975. Orders for 10 plus 26 options had been placed by beginning of 1975.

Notes: The VFW 614 is being manufactured as a collaborative venture under the leadership of VFW-Fokker, participants including the Dutch Fokker-VFW concern and the Belgian SABCA and Fairey companies. The VFW 614 is intended as an ultra-short-haul DC-3 replacement, and an unconventional feature is its over-wing engine-pod installation. Emphasis has been placed on flexibility of operation in a wide variety of different environments and with a minimum of maintenance. Certification was confirmed on August 23, 1974.

VFW-FOKKER VFW 614

Dimensions: Span, 70 ft 6½ in (21,50 m); length, 67 ft 7 in (20,60 m); height, 25 ft 8 in (7,84 m); wing area, 688·89 sq ft (64,00 m²).

VOUGHT A-7E CORSAIR II

Country of Origin: USA.

Type: Single-seat shipboard tactical fighter.

Power Plant: One 15,000 lb (6 804 kg) Allison TF41-A-2 (Rolls-Royce RB. 168-62 Spey) turbofan.

Performance: Max. speed without external stores, 699 mph (1 125 km/h) or Mach 0·92 at sea level, with 12 250-lb (113,4-kg) bombs, 633 mph (1 020 km/h) or Mach 0·87 at sea level; tactical radius with 12 250-lb (113,4-kg) bombs for hi-lo-hi mission at average cruise of 532 mph (856 km/h) with 1 hr on station, 512 mls (825 km); ferry range on internal fuel, 2,775 mls (4 465 km).

Weights: Empty equipped, 17,569 lb (7 969 kg); max. take-off, 42,000+ lb (19 050+ kg).

Armament: One 20-mm M-61A-1 rotary cannon with 1,000 rounds and (for short-range interdiction) maximum ordnance load of 20,000 lb (9 072 kg) distributed between eight external stores stations.

Status: A-7E first flown November 25, 1968, with production deliveries to US Navy following mid-1969. First 67 delivered with Pratt & Whitney TF30-P-8 turbofan (and subsequently redesignated as A-7Cs). Planned procurement totals 706 aircraft.

Notes: A-7E is the shipboard equivalent of the USAF's A-7D (see 1970 edition). Preceded into service by A-7A (199 built) and A-7B (196 built) with 11,350 lb (5 150 kg) TF30-P-6 and 12,200 lb (5 534 kg) TF30-P-8 respectively. Eighty-one early single-seat Corsairs (40 A-7Bs and 41 A-7Cs) are being converted as tandem two-seat TA-7Cs for the training role, these retaining combat capability.

VOUGHT A-7E CORSAIR II

Dimensions: Span, 38 ft 8¾ in (11,80 m); length, 46 ft 1½ in (14,06 m); height, 16 ft 0¾ in (4,90 m); wing area, 375 sq ft (34,83 m²).

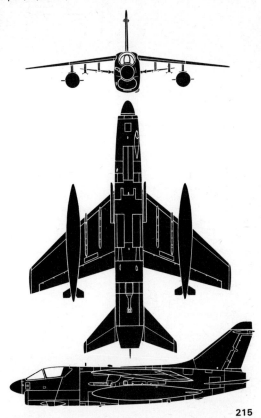

WSK-MIELEC M-15

Country of Origin: Poland.
Type: Agricultural biplane.
Power Plant: One 3,307 lb (1 500 kg) Ivchenko AI-25 turbofan.
Performance: (Estimated) Max. cruise, 168 mph (270 km/h); normal operating speeds, 87–112 mph (140–180 km/h); max. range, 620 mls (1 000 km) at 9,840 ft (3 000 m); initial climb, 964 ft/min (4,9 m/sec); max. climb, 1,673 ft/min (8,5 m/sec).
Weights: Empty, 5,291 lb (2 400 kg); max. take-off, 12,456 lb (5 650 kg).
Status: First aerodynamic prototype (LLM-15) flown July 1973 and second prototype following mid-1974, with planned production deliveries commencing (to the Soviet Union) late 1975–early 1976.
Notes: The world's first turbojet-driven biplane, the M-15 is an agricultural aircraft of radical concept evolved by a joint Polish-Soviet design team. The cockpit provides accommodation for a single pilot, but provision is made in the centre section of the fuselage pod for transportation of an engineer. Twin chemical containers are mounted between the upper and lower wings and these have a total capacity of 638 Imp gal (2 900 l) or 4,850 lb (2 200 kg) of liquid or powdered materials. Air is tapped from the turbofan's low-pressure compressor to drive the agricultural equipment in the tail of the fuselage pod and in the rear portion of the lower wing. An aerodynamic prototype, the LLM-15, was employed to evaluate the basic M-15 configuration in flight.

WSK-MIELEC M-15

Dimensions: Span, 72 ft 2⅛ in (22,00 m); length, 41 ft 1⅓ in (12,53 m); height, 17 ft 0¾ in (5,20 m); wing area, 723·33 sq ft (67,20 m²).

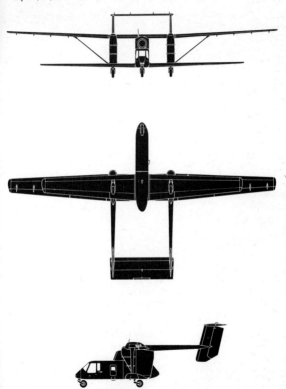

YAKOVLEV YAK-40 (CODLING)

Country of Origin: USSR.

Type: Short-range commercial feederliner.

Power Plant: Three 3,307 lb (1 500 kg) Ivchenko AI-25 turbofans.

Performance: Max. speed, 373 mph (600 km/h) at sea level, 466 mph (750 km/h) at 17,000 ft (5 180 m); max. cruise, 342 mph (550 km/h) at 19,685 ft (6 000 m); econ. cruise, 310 mph (500 km/h) at 32,810 ft (10 000 m); range with 5,070-lb (2 300-kg) payload at econ. cruise, 620 mls (1 000 km), with 3,140-lb (1 425-kg) payload and max. fuel, 920 mls (1 480 km); initial climb, 2,000 ft/min (10,16 m/sec); service ceiling at max. loaded weight, 38,715 ft (11 800 m).

Weights: Empty equipped, 19,865–21,715 lb (9 010–9 850 kg); normal take-off, 27,250–34,170 lb (12 360–15 500 kg); max. take-off, 36,375 lb (16 500 kg).

Accommodation: Flight crew of two, and alternative arrangements for 27 or 34 passengers in three-abreast rows. High-density arrangement for 40 passengers in four-abreast rows, and executive configuration for 8–10 passengers.

Status: First of five prototypes flown October 21, 1966, and first production deliveries (to Aeroflot) mid-1968, the 500th example being completed on February 15, 1974.

Notes: A thrust reverser introduced as standard on centre engine during 1971 when more powerful version with three 3,858 lb (1 750 kg) AI-25T turbofans and increased fuel capacity announced for 1974 delivery as the Yak-40V. The uprated power plant is already installed in Yak-40s serving in the liaison role with the Soviet Air Forces.

YAKOVLEV YAK-40 (CODLING)

Dimensions: Span, 82 ft $0\frac{1}{4}$ in (25,00 m); length, 66 ft $9\frac{1}{2}$ in (20,36 m); height, 21 ft 4 in (6,50 m); wing area, 753·473 sq ft (70 m²).

YAKOVLEV YAK-42

Country of Origin: USSR.

Type: Short- to medium-haul commercial transport.

Power Plant: Three 14,200 lb (6 440 kg) Lotarev B-36 turbofans.

Performance: (Estimated) Max. cruise, 540 mph (870 km/h); econ. cruise, 509 mph (820 km/h) at 26,250 ft (8 000 m); range (with max. payload of 30,850 lb/14 000 kg), 1,118 mls (1 800 km).

Weights: Max. take-off, 110,230 lb (50 000 kg).

Accommodation: Flight crew of two and max. of 120 passengers in single-class six-abreast seating, or mixed-class arrangement for 40 first-class and 60 tourist-class passengers.

Status: First of three prototypes expected to commence flight test programme late 1975 with route-proving trials by Aeroflot scheduled to commence 1977–78.

Notes: Retaining a close family resemblance to the Yak-40 (see pages 218–19), the Yak-42 emphasises simplicity of operation and the ability to utilise restricted airfields with poor surfaces and limited facilities in the remoter areas of the Soviet Union. Aeroflot possesses a requirement for up to 2,000 transports in this category in the 1980–90 timescale.

YAKOVLEV YAK-42

Dimensions: Span, 114 ft 10 in (35,00 m); length, 114 ft 10 in (35,00 m).

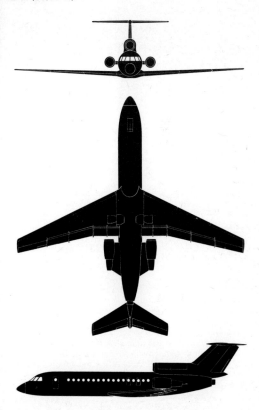

AÉROSPATIALE SA 315B LAMA

Country of Origin: France.
Type: Five-seat light utility helicopter.
Power Plant: One 870 shp (derated to 550 shp) Turboméca Artouste IIIB turboshaft.
Performance: Max. speed, 130 mph (210 km/h) at sea level; max. cruise, 119 mph (192 km/h), with slung load, 75 mph (120 km/h); max. inclined climb rate, 1,319 ft/min (6,7 m/sec); hovering ceiling (in ground effect), 8,530 ft (2 600 m), (out of ground effect), 1,312 ft (400 m); range (at 3,858 lb/1 750 kg), 317 mls (510 km) at sea level, 373 mls (600 km) at 9,840 ft (3 000 m).
Weights: Empty, 2,193 lb (995 kg); max. take-off, 4,850 lb (2 200 kg).
Dimensions: Rotor diam, 36 ft 1¾ in (11,02 m); fuselage length, 33 ft 8 in (10,26 m).
Notes: Flown for the first time on March 17, 1969, the Lama combines features of the SA 318C Alouette II (see 1973 edition) and the SA 319A Alouette III (see 1974 edition), having the airframe of the former (with some reinforcement) and the dynamic components of the latter. Developed primarily to meet the requirements of the Indian armed forces, the Lama is manufactured under licence by Hindustan Aeronautics as the Cheetah (illustrated above). The Lama can transport an external load of 2,204 lb (1 000 kg) at an altitude of more than 8,200 ft (2 500 m).

222

AÉROSPATIALE SA 330 PUMA

Country of Origin: France.
Type: Medium transport helicopter.
Power Plant: Two 1,320 shp Turboméca Turmo III C4 turbo-shafts.
Performance: Max. Speed, 174 mph (280 km/h) at sea level; max. cruise, 165 mph (265 km/h); max. inclined climb, 1,400 ft/min (7,1 m/sec); hovering ceiling (in ground effect), 9,186 ft (2 800 m), (out of ground effect), 6,233 ft (1 900 m); max. range, 390 mls (630 km).
Weights: Empty, 7,561 lb (3 430 kg); max. take-off, 14,110 (6 400 kg).
Dimensions: Rotor diam, 49 ft 2½ on (15,00 m), fuselage length, 46 ft 1½ in (14,06 m).
Notes: The Puma is being built under a joint production agreement between Aérospatiale and Westland, the first to be assembled by the latter concern flying on November 25, 1970. The Puma can accommodate 16–20 troops or up to 5,511 lb (2 500 kg) of cargo, and 40 are being delivered to the RAF for the assault role, 130 having been ordered by French Army Aviation. The Puma has been supplied to the Portuguese, South African, Zaïre Rep., Abu Dhabian, Algerian, and Ivory Coast air arms, and a commercial version, the SA 330F (illustrated above) with 1,385 shp Turmo IVA turbo-shafts, obtained FAA Type Approval in 1971, this carrying 15–17 passengers over 217 mls (350 km).

AÉROSPATIALE SA 341 GAZELLE

Country of Origin: France.
Type: Five-seat light utility helicopter.
Power Plant: One 592 shp Turboméca Astazou IIIN turbo-shaft.
Performance: Max. speed, 165 mph (265 km/h) at sea level; max. cruise, 149 mph (240 km/h); max. inclined climb rate, 1,214 ft/min (6,16 m/sec); hovering ceiling (in ground effect), 10,170 ft (3 100 m), (out of ground effect), 8,530 ft (2 600 m); max. range, 403 mls (650 km).
Weights: Empty, 1,873 lb (850 kg); max. take-off, 3,747 lb (1 700 kg).
Dimensions: Rotor diam, 34 ft $5\frac{1}{2}$ in (10,50 m); fuselage length, 31 ft $2\frac{3}{4}$ in (9,52 m).
Notes: Intended as a successor to the Alouette II, the Gazelle is being built under a joint production agreement between Aérospatiale and Westland. Two prototypes and four pre-production Gazelles were flown, and the first production example flew on August 6, 1971. The Gazelle is to be operated in the LOH (Light Observation Helicopter) role by both the French (SA 341F) and British armed forces (SA 341B for the Army, SA 341C for the Navy and SA 341D for the RAF), and it is anticipated that these will respectively purchase some 170 and 250 Gazelles. Licence production is being undertaken in Yugoslavia and deliveries commenced late 1973.

AÉROSPATIALE SA 360 DAUPHIN

Country of Origin: France.
Type: Multi-purpose and transport helicopter.
Power Plant: One 1,025 shp (derated to 878 shp) Turboméca Astazou XVIIIA turboshaft.
Performance: Max. cruise, 171 mph (275 km/h); econ. cruise, 143 mph (230 km/h); inclined climb rate (at 5,500 lb/2 500 kg), 1,476 ft/min (7,5 m/sec); hovering ceiling (in ground effect), 15,584 ft (4 750 m), (out of ground effect), 14,107 ft (4 300 m); range (with 2,204-lb/1 000-kg payload), 62 mls (100 km), (with 1,323-lb/600-kg payload), 466 mls (750 km).
Weights: Empty equipped, 2,976 lb (1 350 kg); max. takeoff, 5,952 lb (2 700 kg).
Dimensions: Rotor diam, 37 ft 8¾ in (11,50 m); fuselage length, 36 ft 4 in (11,08 m).
Notes: Intended as a successor to the Alouette III, the SA 360 utilises a semi-rigid four-blade rotor and a ducted 11-blade tail rotor. The two prototypes made their initial flights on June 2, 1972, and January 29, 1973, respectively, and the first production example is scheduled for delivery mid-1976. A twin-engined derivative, the SA 365, is under development with two 681 shp Turboméca Arriel free turbines and an optional retractable undercarriage. A projected variant is the SA 366 with two 582 shp Avco Lycoming LTS 101 turboshafts.

AGUSTA A 109C HIRUNDO

Country of Origin: Italy.

Type: Eight-seat utility helicopter.

Power Plant: Two 400 shp Allison 250-C20 turboshafts.

Performance: (At 4,850 lb/2 200 kg) Max. speed, 169 mph (272 km/h) at sea level; econ. cruise, 139 mph (223 km/h) at sea level; max. inclined climb, 2,067 ft/min (10,5 m/sec); hovering ceiling (in ground effect), 11,810 ft (3 600 m), (out of ground effect), 9,190 ft (2 800 m); max. range, 457 mls (735 km) at 6,560 ft (2 000 m).

Weights: Empty, 2,645 lb (1 200 kg); max. take-off, 5,291 lb (2 400 kg).

Dimensions: Rotor diam, 36 ft 1 in (11,00 m); fuselage length, 36 ft 7 in (11,14 m).

Notes: The first of four Hirundo (Swallow) prototypes flew on August 4, 1971. This was lost as a result of resonance problems, flight trials being resumed with the second and third prototypes early 1973. The first production examples are scheduled to be delivered during 1975. The Hirundo is intended to fit between the licence-built Bell 206 JetRanger and Bell 212 in the Agusta helicopter range, and carries a pilot and seven passengers in its basic form. It is also suitable for the ambulance role, accommodating two casualty stretchers and two medical attendants when the forward cabin bulkhead is removed, and for freight carrying the forward row of passenger seats may be removed.

BELL MODEL 205A (IROQUOIS)

Country of Origin: USA.

Type: Fifteen-seat utility helicopter.

Power Plant: One 1,400 shp Lycoming T5313A turboshaft.

Performance: (At 9,500 lb/4 309 kg) Max. speed, 127 mph (204 km/h) at sea level; max. cruise, 111 mph (179 km/h) at 8,000 ft (2 440 m); max. inclined climb, 1,680 ft/min (8,53 m/sec); hovering ceiling (in ground effect), 10,400 ft (3 170 m), (out of ground effect), 6,000 ft (1 830 m); range, 344 mls (553 km) at 8,000 ft (2 440 m).

Weights: Empty equipped, 5,082 lb (2 305 kg); normal take-off, 9,500 lb (4 309 kg).

Dimensions: Rotor diam, 48 ft 0 in (14,63 m); fuselage length, 41 ft 6 in (12,65 m).

Notes: The Model 205A is basically similar to the Model 204B (see 1973 edition) but introduces a longer fuselage with increased cabin space. It is produced under licence in Italy by Agusta as the AB 205, and is assembled under licence in Formosa (Taiwan). The initial version for the US Army, the UH-1D, had a 1,100 shp T53-L-11 turboshaft. This model was manufactured under licence in Federal Germany. The UH-1D has been succeeded in production for the US Army by the UH-1H with a 1,400 shp T53-L-13 turboshaft, and a similar helicopter for the Mobile Command of the Canadian Armed Forces is designated CUH-1H. A progressive development is the Model 214 (see page 232).

BELL MODEL 206B JETRANGER II

Country of Origin: USA.
Type: Five-seat light utility helicopter.
Power Plant: One 400 shp Allison 250-C20 turboshaft.
Performance: (At 3,000 lb/1 361 kg) Max. cruise, 136 mph (219 km/h) at sea level, 142 mph (228 km/h) at 5,000 ft (1 524 m); hovering ceiling (in ground effect), 13,200 ft (4 023 m), (out of ground effect), 8,700 ft (2 652 m); max. inclined climb, 1,540 ft/min (7,82 m/sec); max. range, 436 mls (702 km) at 10,000 ft (3 048 m).
Weights: Empty, 1,455 lb (660 kg); max. take-off, 3,000 lb (1 360 kg).
Dimensions: Rotor diam, 33 ft 4 in (10,16 m); fuselage length, 31 ft 2 in (9,50 m).
Notes: The JetRanger is manufactured in both commercial and military versions, and the current production variant, the Model 206B JetRanger II, differs from the Model 206A Jet-Ranger in having an uprated turboshaft. A light observation version for the US Army is known as the OH-58A Kiowa, and a training version for the US Navy is known as the TH-57A SeaRanger. An Australian-built version of the Model 206B is being delivered to the Australian Army, and this helicopter is also built in Italy by Agusta as the AB 206B-1. The OH-58A Kiowa has a larger main rotor of 35 ft 4 in (10,77 m) diameter and a fuselage of 32 ft 3½ in (9,84 m) length.

BELL MODEL 206L LONG RANGER

Country of Origin: USA.

Type: Seven-seat light utility helicopter.

Power Plant: One 420 shp Allison 250-C20B turboshaft.

Performance: (At 3,900 lb/1 769 kg) Max. speed, 144 mph (232 km/h); cruise, 136 mph (229 km/h) at sea level; hovering ceiling (in ground effect), 8,200 ft (2 499 m), (out of ground effect), 2,000 ft (610 m); range, 390 mls (628 km) at sea level, 430 mls (692 km) at 5,000 ft (1 524 m).

Weights: Empty, 1,861 lb (844 kg); max. take-off, 3,900 lb (1 769 kg).

Dimensions: Rotor diam. 37 ft 0 in (11,28 m); fuselage length, 33 ft 3 in (10,13 m).

Notes: The Model 206L Long Ranger is a stretched and more powerful version of the Model 206B JetRanger II, with a longer fuselage, increased fuel capacity, an uprated engine and a larger rotor. The Long Ranger is to be manufactured in parallel with the JetRanger II with initial customer deliveries scheduled for early 1975, prototype testing having been initiated during the course of 1973. The Long Ranger will be available with emergency flotation gear and with a 2,000-lb (907-kg) capacity cargo hook. Cabin volume is 83 cu ft (2,35 m³) as compared with the 49 cu ft (1,39 m³) of the JetRanger II (see page 228). By 1975, more than 4,000 commercial and military examples of the basic JetRanger series had been delivered.

BELL MODEL 209 HUEYCOBRA

Country of Origin: USA.

Type: Two-seat attack helicopter.

Power Plant: One 1,800 shp Pratt & Whitney (UACL) T400-CP-400 coupled turboshaft.

Performance: Max. speed, 207 mph (333 km/h) at sea level; max. range (without reserves, 359 mls (577 km); max. inclined climb, 1,090 ft/min (5,54 m/sec); hovering ceiling (in ground effect), 12,450 ft (3 794 m).

Weights: Operational (including crew), 6,816 lb (3 091 kg); max. take-off, 10,000 lb (4 535 kg).

Dimensions: Rotor diam, 44 ft 0 in (13,41 m); fuselage length, 44 ft 7 in (13,59 m).

Notes: The version of the Model 209 HueyCobra described above is employed by the US Marine Corps as the AH-1J SeaCobra, differing from the US Army's AH-1G primarily in having a "Twin Pac" power plant. Eighty-nine AH-1Js are being procured by the USMC from funding up to and including Fiscal 1974 with procurement of a further 35 planned, and 202 examples are being supplied to Iran with deliveries commencing May 1974. By comparison with the AH-1G, the AH-1J has an improved armament system embodying a three-barrelled 20-mm XM-197 cannon in a chin turret. Four external stores attachment points under the stub-wings can carry a variety of ordnance loads, including Minigun pods and rocket packs.

BELL MODEL 212 TWIN TWO-TWELVE

Country of Origin: USA.

Type: Fifteen-seat utility helicopter.

Power Plant: One 1,800 shp Pratt & Whitney PT6T-3 coupled turboshaft.

Performance: Max. speed, 121 mph (194 km/h) at sea level; max. inclined climb at 10,000 lb (4 535 kg), 1,460 ft/min (7,4 m/sec); hovering ceiling (in ground effect), 17,100 ft (5 212 m), (out of ground effect), 9,900 ft (3 020 m); max. range, 296 mls (476 km) at sea level.

Weights: Empty, 5,500 lb (2 495 kg); max. take-off, 10,000 lb (4 535 kg).

Dimensions: Rotor diam, 48 ft 2½ in (14,69 m); fuselage length, 42 ft 10¾ in (13,07 m).

Notes: The Model 212 is based on the Model 205 (see page 227) from which it differs primarily in having a twin-engined power plant (two turboshaft engines coupled to a combining gearbox with a single output shaft), and both commercial and military versions are being produced. A model for the Canadian Armed Forces is designated CUH-1N, and an essentially similar variant of the Model 212, the UH-1N, is being supplied to the USAF, the USN, and the USMC. All versions of the Model 212 can carry an external load of 4,400 lb (1 814 kg), and can maintain cruise performance on one engine component at maximum gross weight.

BELL MODEL 214

Country of Origin: USA.

Type: Sixteen-seat utility helicopter.

Power Plant: One 2,930 shp Avco Lycoming T55-L-7C turboshaft.

Performance: Max. speed, 190 mph (305 km/h) at sea level; max. cruise (at gross weight of 13,000 lb/5 897 kg), 150 mph (241 km/h); range, 300 mls (483 km).

Weights: Normal max. take-off, 13,000 lb (5 897 kg), (with slung load), 15,000 lb (6 804 kg).

Dimensions: Rotor diam, 50 ft 0 in (15,20 m).

Notes: Development of the Model 214, originally known as the HueyPlus, was initiated in 1970 as a progressive development of the Model 205 (UH-1H). Utilising an essentially similar airframe with strengthened main beams, pylon structure and aft fuselage, and the main rotor and tail rotor drive systems of the Model 309 KingCobra (see 1973 edition) coupled with the Lycoming T55-L-7C turboshaft installed in the second KingCobra, this utility helicopter is being developed for military use as the Model 214A and will be certificated for commercial use as the Model 214B (Avco Lycoming LTC4B-8D). First flight of the Model 214A was scheduled for early 1974, and first deliveries against orders from the Iranian Government for 287 helicopters of this type are scheduled for February 1975, at which time the Model 214B will be certificated.

BELL MODEL 222

Country of Origin: USA.

Type: Eight/twelve-seat commercial utility helicopter.

Power Plant: Two 592 shp Avco Lycoming LTS-101-650C turboshafts.

Performance: (Estimated) Max. speed, 180 mph (290 km/h); cruise, 150 mph (241 km/h); range (with 30 min. reserves), 425 mls (684 km).

Weights: Normal max. take-off, 6,700 lb (3 039 kg).

Dimensions: Max. length, 39 ft 9 in (12,12 m).

Notes: The first Bell helicopter designed from the outset for the commercial market, the Model 222 business and utility helicopter is to be offered in six-passenger executive and 10-passenger high-density configurations, and will have a payload of 2,730 lb (1 238 kg). The decision to proceed with development of the Model 222 was taken in April 1974, and the prototype is currently scheduled to commence its flight test programme late 1975 with initial production deliveries anticipated for 1978. Of advanced aerodynamic design, with fully-retractable tricycle undercarriage and rubber-mounted rotor pylon and engine to isolate structure-borne vibration, the Model 222 is adaptable for a variety of roles, including that of ambulance in which form it will accommodate two stretcher patients and two medical attendants. In cargo configuration, the Model 222 will have a volume of 124 cu ft (3,5 m³) and a starboard cargo door.

BELL MODEL 409 (YAH-63)

Country of Origin: USA.

Type: Tandem two-seat attack helicopter.

Power Plant: Two 1,500 shp General Electric YT700-GE-700 turboshafts.

Performance: No details available for publication.

Weights: (Estimated) Empty, 10,000 lb (4 536 kg); normal max. take-off, 14,000 lb (6 350 kg).

Dimensions: No details available for publication.

Notes: The Model 409 is one of two designs selected by the US Army from five proposals to meet the requirements of the service's AAH (Advanced Attack Helicopter) system, a contract for two flying prototypes and a ground test specimen having been placed on June 22, 1973, under the designation YAH-63. The first YAH-63 is scheduled to enter the flight test phase in March 1975, and to participate in a competitive fly-off with the Hughes YAH-64 (see page 239) one year later. This phase of the programme is expected to be completed in June 1976 when selection of one of the two competing helicopters will be made. Embodying extensive armour and with blast-proof glass shields separating the cockpits, the YAH-63 features a turret-mounted triple-barrel 30-mm XM-188 rotary cannon beneath the fuselage nose, the gunner being seated in the aft cockpit. For the primary mission eight BGM-71A TOW anti-tank missiles will be carried on small stub wings.

BOEING VERTOL MODEL 114

Country of Origin: USA.

Type: Medium transport helicopter.

Power Plant: (CH-47C) Two 3,750 shp Lycoming T55-L-11 turboshafts.

Performance: (CH-47C at 33,000 lb/14 969 kg) Max. speed, 190 mph (306 km/h) at sea level; average cruise, 158 mph (254 km/h); max. inclined climb, 2,880 ft/min (14,63 m/sec); hovering ceiling (out of ground effect), 14,750 ft (4 495 m); mission radius, 115 mls (185 km).

Weights: Empty, 20,378 lb (9 243); max. take-off, 46,000 lb (20 865 kg).

Dimensions: Rotor diam (each), 60 ft 0 in (18,29 m); fuselage length, 51 ft 0 in (15,54 m).

Notes: The Model 114 is the standard medium transport helicopter of the US Army, and is operated by that service under the designation CH-47 Chinook. The initial production model, the CH-47A, was powered by 2,200 shp T55-L-5 or 2,650 shp T55-L-7 turboshafts. This was succeeded by the CH-47B with 2,850 shp T55-L-7C engines, redesigned rotor blades and other modifications, and this, in turn, gave place to the current CH-47C with more powerful engines, strengthened transmissions, and increased fuel capacity. This model is manufactured in Italy by Elicotteri Meriodionali, orders calling for 24 (of 26) for the Italian Army and 18 (of 42) for the Iranian Army.

235

BOEING VERTOL MODEL 179 (YUH-61A)

Country of Origin: USA.

Type: Tactical transport helicopter.

Power Plant: Two 1,536 shp General Electric YT700-GE-700 turboshafts.

Performance: Max. cruise, 185 mph (298 km/h); normal cruise, 170 mph (274 km/h); mission range, 450–700 mls (724–1 126 km).

Weights: Max. take-off, 18,700 lb (8 482 kg).

Dimensions: Rotor diam., 49 ft 0 in (14,93 m); fuselage length, 51 ft 8¾ in (15,77 m).

Notes: The YUH-61A is one of two finalists in the US Army's UTTAS (Utility Tactical Transport Aircraft System) contest, one static test example and three flying prototypes having been ordered, the first of the latter having flown on November 29, 1974. A fourth flying prototype is being built as a company-owned demonstrator, the Boeing Vertol Company planning to market a commercial 14–25 passenger version. The YUH-61A is competing with the Sikorsky YUH-60A (see page 240) as a successor to the Bell UH-1H Iroquois in the troop transportation, casevac and logistics support roles, and a competitive evaluation of the two helicopter types is to be conducted by the US Army from late 1975 which is aimed at selecting one for production from March 1977. The YUH-61A can carry a 10,000-lb (4 536 kg) slung load and is transportable by C-130 Hercules.

BOEING VERTOL MODEL 301 (XCH-62)

Country of Origin: USA.

Type: Heavy lift helicopter.

Power Plant: Three 8,079 shp Allison XT701-AD-700 turboshafts.

Performance: (Estimated) Max. speed (with a 45,000-lb/ 20 412-kg external load), 175 mph (282 km/h); ferry range (at max. gross weight), 1,730 mls (2 784 km); hovering ceiling (in ground effect), 12,200 ft (3 720 m).

Weights: Empty, 59,580 lb (27 025 kg); design gross, 118,000 lb (53 520 kg); max. take-off, 148,000 lb (67 130 kg).

Dimensions: Rotor diam. (each), 92 ft 0 in (28,04 m); fuselage length, 89 ft 3 in (27,20 m).

Notes: The XCH-62 is being developed to flight test status under a US Army contract awarded on May 11, 1971, as the first phase of an HLH (Heavy Lift Helicopter) development programme, and the sole prototype is scheduled to commence its flight test programme in August 1975. Application has been made to the FAA by the Boeing Vertol Company for commercial certification of the helicopter. The primary mission of the XCH-62 is to carry a 45,000-lb (20 412-kg) load for two 28-mile (46-km) radius round-trip missions. Twelve troops may be accommodated in the cargo compartment and the crew comprises four members. The prototype is essentially an advanced technology demonstrator.

ENSTROM 280 SHARK

Country of Origin: USA.

Type: Three-seat light utility helicopter.

Power Plant: One 205 hp Avco Lycoming HIO-360-CIA four-cylinder horizontally-opposed engine.

Performance: Max. cruise, 110 mph (177 km/h); hovering ceiling (in ground effect), 5,600 ft (1 707 m); normal range, 247 mls (397 km), (with optional 33 Imp gal/150 l fuel tank), 330 mls (531 km); max. endurance, 3 hrs.

Weights: Max. take-off, 2,400 lb (1 089 kg).

Dimensions: Rotor diam., 32 ft 0 in (9,75 m); max. length, 30 ft 6 in (9,29 m).

Notes: The Shark is a restyled and aerodynamically improved version of the Enstrom F.28A which, in turn, was an improved version of the F.28 originally certificated in 1965. Customer deliveries of the Shark were expected to commence early 1975, and production of the F.28A and Shark is expected to attain 156 helicopters during the course of the year, 30 per cent of these being of the later model. Retaining the basic dynamic components of the F.28A, the Shark has optional increased fuel tankage and swept vertical tail surfaces for improved control during turns and autorotation. A turbo-supercharged version of the basic helicopter, the Turbo-Shark, is expected to be certificated during the course of 1975, and a heavy-duty utility version is under development.

HUGHES YAH-64

Country of Origin: USA.
Type: Tandem two-seat attack helicopter.
Power Plant: Two 1,500 shp General Electric YT700-GE-700 turboshafts.
Performance: No details available for publication.
Weights: Empty, 9,500 lb (4 309 kg); typical take-off (with eight TOW missiles), 13,600 lb (6 169 kg).
Dimensions: No details available for publication.
Notes: Competing with the Bell YAH-63 (see page 234) in the US Army contest for an AAH (Advanced Attack Helicopter) system, the YAH-64 was ordered (two flying prototypes and a ground test specimen) on June 22, 1973, and is scheduled to commence its test programme in March 1975. It will subsequently participate in a competitive fly-off with the YAH-63, the winning contender being awarded production orders. The YAH-64 has a single-barrel 30-mm gun, which, based on the chain-driven bolt system and having 800 rounds, is suspended beneath the forward fuselage, the gunner occupying the forward cockpit. For the primary mission, the YAH-64 carries eight BGM-71A TOW (Tube-launched Optically-tracked Wire-guided) anti-tank missiles. A swivelling electro-optical turret in the nose contains optical and forward-looking infra-red sights. The stub wings may be fitted with four ordnance pylons, those outboard carrying the TOW missiles.

KAMOV KA-25 (HORMONE A)

Country of Origin: USSR.

Type: Shipboard anti-submarine warfare helicopter.

Power Plant: Two 900 shp Glushenkov GTD-3 turboshafts.

Performance: (Estimated) Max. speed, 130 mph (209 km/h); normal cruise, 120 mph (193 km/h); max. range, 400 mls (644 km); service ceiling, 11,000 ft (3 353 m).

Weights: (Estimated) Empty, 10,500 lb (4 765 kg); max. take-off, 16,500 lb (7 484 kg).

Dimensions: Rotor diam (each), 51 ft 7½ in (15,74 m); approx. fuselage length, 35 ft 6 in (10,82 m).

Notes: Possessing a basically similar airframe to that of the Ka-25K (see 1973 edition) and employing a similar self-contained assembly comprising rotors, transmission, engines and auxiliaries, the Ka-25 serves with the Soviet Navy primarily in the ASW role but is also employed in the utility and transport roles. The ASW Ka-25 serves aboard the helicopter cruisers *Moskva* and *Leningrad* as well as with shore-based units. A search radar installation is mounted in a nose radome, but other sensor housings and antennae differ widely from helicopter to helicopter. There is no evidence that externally-mounted weapons may be carried. Each landing wheel is surrounded by an inflatable pontoon surmounted by inflation bottles. Sufficient capacity is available to accommodate up to a dozen personnel. The commercial Ka-25K can be employed in the flying crane role.

MBB BO 105

Country of Origin: Federal Germany.
Type: Five/six-seat light utility helicopter.
Power Plant: Two 400 shp Allison 250-C20 turboshafts.
Performance: Max. speed, 155 mph (250 km/h) at sea level; max. cruise, 138 mph (222 km/h); max. inclined climb, 1,870 ft/min (9,5 m/sec); hovering ceiling (in ground effect), 7,610 ft (2 320 m), (out of ground effect), 5,085 ft (1 550 m); normal range, 388 mls (625 km) at 5,000 ft (1 525 m).
Weights: Empty, 2,360 lb (1 070 kg); normal take-off, 4,630 lb (2 100 kg); max. take-off, 5,070 lb (2 300 kg).
Dimensions: Rotor diam, 32 ft 1¾ in (9,80 m); fuselage length, 28 ft 0½ in (8,55 m).
Notes: The BO 105 features a rigid unarticulated main rotor with folding glass-fibre reinforced plastic blades, and the first prototype (with a conventional rotor) was tested in 1966, three prototypes being followed by four pre-production examples, and production deliveries commencing during 1971. The German armed forces have acquired examples for evaluation. The third prototype was powered by 375 shp MTU 6022 turboshafts, but the production model has standardised on the Allison 250. Production is undertaken by the Siebelwerke-ATG subsidiary of MBB and some 140 BO 105s had been flown by the beginning of 1975. A seven-seat derivative, the BO 106, was flown on September 25, 1973.

MIL MI-8 (HIP)

Country of Origin: USSR.

Type: General-purpose transport helicopter.

Power Plant: Two 1,500 shp Izotov TV-2-117A turboshafts.

Performance: (At 24,470 lb/11 100 kg) Max. speed, 155 mph (250 km/h); max. cruise, 140 mph (225 km/h); hovering ceiling (in ground effect), 5,900 ft (1 800 m), (out of ground effect), 2,625 ft (800 m); service ceiling, 14,760 ft (4 500 m); range with 6,615 lb (3 000 kg) of freight, 264 mls (425 km).

Weights: Empty (cargo), 15,787 lb (7 171 kg), (passenger), 16,352 lb (7 417 kg); normal take-off, 24,470 lb (11 100 kg); max. take-off (for VTO), 26,455 lb (12 000 kg).

Dimensions: Rotor diam, 69 ft 10¼ in (21,29 m); fuselage length, 59 ft 7⅓ in (18,17 m).

Notes: The Mi-8 has been in continuous production since 1964 for both civil and military tasks. The standard commercial passenger version has a basic flight crew of two or three and 28 four-abreast seats, and the aeromedical version accommodates 12 casualty stretchers and a medical attendant. As a freighter the Mi-8 will carry up to 8,818 lb (4 000 kg) of cargo, and military tasks include assault transport, search and rescue, and anti-submarine warfare. The Mi-8 is now operated by several Warsaw Pact air forces, serving primarily in the support transport role, and has been exported to numerous countries, including Finland, Pakistan and Egypt.

MIL MI-24 (HIND)

Country of Origin: USSR.

Type: Gunship and assault transport helicopter.

Power Plant: Two (approx.) 1,500 shp Isotov turboshafts.

Performance: (Estimated) Max. speed, 160 mph (257 km/h); max. cruise, 140 mph (225 km/h); hovering ceiling (in ground effect), 6,000 ft (1 830 m), (out of ground effect), 1,600 ft (790 m); normal range, 300 mls (480 km).

Weights: Normal loaded, 25,000 lb (11 340 kg).

Dimensions: Rotor diam., 55 ft 0 in (16,76 m); fuselage length, 55 ft 6 in (16,90 m).

Notes: Employed in considerable numbers by the Soviet forces, the Mi-24 is apparently serving in two versions. One version (*Hind-A*), illustrated above, has three weapons stations on each auxiliary wing, the two inboard stations carrying UV-32-57 rocket pods and the outboard station taking the form of a vertical extension of the wingtip with a double carrier for two AT-3 *Sagger* wire-guided anti-tank missiles. The other version (*Hind-B*) does not have the wing-tip vertical extensions. Both versions have a 12,7-mm machine gun in the extreme fuselage nose, armour protection for the flight crew and accommodation for 8–12 assault troops with a large door aft of the flight deck on each side enabling them to exit rapidly. The Mi-24 may utilise some of the components of the Mi-8 (see opposite page) but appears to be somewhat smaller.

SIKORSKY S-61A

Country of Origin: USA.

Type: Amphibious transport and rescue helicopter.

Power Plant: (S-61A-4) Two 1,500 shp General Electric T58-GE-5 turboshafts.

Performance: (At 20,500 lb/9 300 kg) Max. speed, 153 mph (248 km/h); range cruise, 126 mph (203 km/h); max. inclined climb, 2,200 ft/min (11,17 m/sec); hovering ceiling (in ground effect), 8,600 ft (2 820 m); range with max. fuel and 10 % reserves, 525 mls (845 km).

Weights: Empty, 9,763 lb (4 428 kg); normal take-off, 20,500 lb (9 300 kg); max., 21,500 lb (9 750 kg).

Dimensions: Rotor diam, 62 ft 0 in (18,90 m); fuselage length, 54 ft 9 in (16,69 m).

Notes: A transport equivalent of the S-61D (see page 245) with sonar, weapons, and automatic blade folding deleted, and a cargo floor inserted, the S-61A is used by the USAF for missile site support as the CH-3B, this having 1,250 shp T58-GE-8Bs and accommodation for 26 troops or 15 stretchers. Eight similarly-powered S-61A-1s supplied to Denmark for the rescue task were supplemented in 1970 by a ninth machine, and 10 T58-GE-5-powered S-61A-4s equipped to carry 31 combat troops and supplied to Malaysia were supplemented during 1971 by six further S-61A-4s. The S-61L and S-61N (see 1967 edition) are non-amphibious and amphibious commercial versions.

SIKORSKY S-61D (SEA KING)

Country of Origin: USA.
Type: Amphibious anti-submarine helicopter.
Power Plant: Two 1,500 shp General Electric T58-GE-10 turboshafts.
Performance: Max. speed, 172 mph (277 km/h) at sea level; inclined climb, 2,200 ft/min (11,2 m/sec); hovering ceiling (out of ground effect), 8,200 ft (2 500 m); range (with 10% reserves), 622 mls (1 000 km).
Weights: Empty equipped, 12,087 lb (5 481 kg); max. take-off, 20,500 lb (9 297 kg).
Dimensions: Rotor diam, 62 ft 0 in (18,90 m); fuselage length, 54 ft 9 in (16,69 m).
Notes: A more powerful derivative of the S-61B, the S-61D serves with the US Navy as the SH-3D, 74 helicopters of this type following on production of 255 SH-3As (S-61Bs) for the ASW role. Licence manufacture of the S-61D (with 1,500 shp Rolls-Royce Gnome turboshafts) is undertaken in the UK by Westland as the Sea King HAS Mk. 1, 56 being delivered to the Royal Navy. Deliveries of the improved Sea King Mk. 50 for the Royal Australian Navy will commence during 1974, and production is being undertaken of a tactical transport version, the Commando (see page 249). Licence manufacture of the S-61D is also being undertaken in Italy by Agusta for the Italian and Iranian navies. The SH-3G and SH-3H are upgraded conversions of the SH-3A.

SIKORSKY S-61R

Country of Origin: USA.
Type: Amphibious transport and rescue helicopter.
Power Plant: (CH-3E) Two 1,500 shp General Electric T58-GE-5 turboshafts.
Performance: (CH-3E at 21,247 lb/9 635 kg) Max. speed, 162 mph (261 km/h) at sea level; range cruise, 144 mph (232 km/h); max. inclined climb, 1,310 ft/min (6,6 m/sec); hovering ceiling (in ground effect), 4,100 ft (1 250 m); range with 10% reserves, 465 mls (748 km).
Weights: (CH-3E) Empty, 13,255 lb (6 010 kg); normal take-off, 21,247 lb (9 635 kg); max. take-off, 22,050 lb (10 000 kg).
Dimensions: Rotor diam, 62 ft 0 in (18,90 m); fuselage length, 57 ft 3 in (17,45 m).
Notes: Although based on the S-61A, the S-61R embodies numerous design changes, including a rear ramp and a tricycle-type undercarriage. Initial model for the USAF was the CH-3C with 1,300 shp T58-GE-1 turboshafts, but this was subsequently updated to CH-3E standards. The CH-3E can accommodate 25–30 troops or 5,000 lb (2 270 kg) of cargo, and may be fitted with a TAT-102 barbette on each sponson mounting a 7,62-mm Minigun. The HH-3E is a USAF rescue version with armour, self-sealing tanks, and refuelling probe, and the HH-3F Pelican (illustrated) is a US Coast Guard search and rescue model.

SIKORSKY S-65 (YCH-53E)

Country of Origin: USA.

Type: Amphibious assault transport helicopter.

Power Plant: Three 4,380 shp General Electric T64-GE-415 turboshafts.

Performance: Max. speed, 200+ mph (322+ km/h); max. cruise, 195 mph (314 km/h).

Weights: Operational empty, 33,000 lb (14 968 kg); max. take-off, 70,000 lb (31 750 kg).

Dimensions: Rotor diam., 79 ft 0 in (24,08 m); fuselage length, 73 ft 5 in (22,38 m).

Notes: The YCH-53E is a growth version of the CH-53D Sea Stallion (see 1974 edition) embodying a third engine, an uprated transmission system, a seventh main rotor blade and increased rotor diameter. The first of two prototypes was flown on March 1, 1974, but a production decision is not anticipated prior to early 1976. The YCH-53E can accommodate up to 56 troops in a high-density arrangement and can lift a 32,000-lb (14 515-kg) external load over a radius of 58 miles (93 km) at sea level in a 90 deg F temperature. The planned production programme envisages the acquisition of 70 helicopters of this type divided equally between the US Navy and US Marine Corps. The YCH-53E offers a major performance advance over earlier members of the S-65 family and is capable of retrieving 93 per cent of USMC tactical aircraft without disassembly.

SIKORSKY S-70 (YUH-60A)

Country of Origin: USA.

Type: Tactical transport helicopter.

Power Plant: Two 1,536 shp General Electric YT700-GE-700 turboshafts.

Performance: Max. speed, 193 mph (310 km/h) at sea level; cruise, 168 mph (270 km/h) at sea level; hovering ceiling (in ground effect), 10,000 ft (3 048 m), (out of ground effect), 5,800 ft (1 768 m); normal range, 460 mls (740 km).

Weights: Max. take-off, 17,520 lb (7 945 kg).

Dimensions: Rotor diam., 53 ft 0 in (16,15 m); fuselage length, 50 ft 11½ in (15,53 m).

Notes: Flown for the first time on October 17, 1974, the YUH-60A is competing with the Boeing Vertol YUH-61A (see page 236) to fulfil the US Army's UTTAS (Utility Tactical Transport Aircraft System) requirement for a successor to the Bell UH-1H Iroquois. The YUH-60A will accommodate four casualty stretchers plus three sitting casualties in the casevac role or up to 11 fully-equipped troops plus a crew of three. A commercial version of the helicopter, the S-70C-20 is currently proposed and a further projected development, the S-70C-29, has a stretched fuselage accommodating up to 29 passengers and sponsons housing retractable main undercarriage members. A company-funded S-70C-20 will fly during 1975. The YUH-60A may be transported by the Lockheed C-130 Hercules.

WESTLAND COMMANDO MK. 2

Country of Origin: United Kingdom (US licence).

Type: Tactical transport helicopter.

Power Plant: Two 1,590 shp Rolls-Royce Gnome 1400-1 turboshafts.

Performance: Max. speed (at 19,900 lb/9 046 kg), 138 mph (222 km/h); max. cruise, 127 mph (204 km/h); max. inclined climb, 1,930 ft/min (9,8 m/sec); range (with 30 troops), 161 mls (259 km); ferry range, 1,036 mls (1 668 km).

Weights: Empty equipped, 11,487–12,122 lb (5 221– 5 510 kg); max. take-off, 20,000 lb (9 072 kg).

Dimensions: Rotor diam, 62 ft 0 in (18,89 m); fuselage length, 54 ft 9 in (16,69 m).

Notes: The Commando is a Westland-developed land-based army support helicopter derivative of the licence-built Sikorsky S-61D Sea King (see page 245), search radar and other specialised items being deleted together with the sponsons which endow the Sea King with amphibious capability. The first five examples completed as Commando Mk. 1s were minimum change conversions of Sea King airframes, the first of these flying on September 12, 1973 (illustrated above), but subsequent Commandos are being built to Mk. 2 standards with the uprated Gnome turboshafts selected for the Sea King Mk. 50s ordered by Australia. The first production Commandos are being built for Egypt for 1975 delivery.

249

WESTLAND WG.13 LYNX

Country of Origin: United Kingdom.

Type: Multi-purpose and transport helicopter.

Power Plant: Two 900 shp Rolls-Royce BS.360-07-26 turboshafts.

Performance: (General purpose versions) Max. speed, 207 mph (333 km/h); max. cruise, 184 mph (296 km/h) at sea level; max. inclined climb, 2,800 ft/min (14,2 m/sec); hovering ceiling (out of ground effect), 12,000 ft (3 650 m); range (with 10 passengers), 173 mls (278 km), (with internal cargo and full tanks), 489 mls (788 km).

Weights: Operational empty, 5,532–6,125 lb (2 509–2 778 kg); max. take-off, 8,000 lb (3 620 kg); overload, 8,840 lb (4 009 kg).

Dimensions: Rotor diam, 42 ft 0 in (12,80 m); fuselage length, 38 ft 3$\frac{1}{4}$ in (11,66 m).

Notes: The Lynx, the first of 12 prototypes of which commenced its flight test programme on March 21, 1971, and the first production machine (a Lynx A.H. Mk. 1 for the British Army) was scheduled to fly at the end of 1973 with the first naval example (a Lynx HR Mk. 2 for the Royal Navy) following mid-1974. Current plans call for the delivery of some 80 examples of an ASW version to France's *Aéronavale*, the Lynx being one of three helicopter types covered by the Anglo-French agreement. A total of 277 is programmed for the British services.

ACKNOWLEDGEMENTS

The author wishes to record his thanks to the following sources of copyright photographs appearing in this volume: Aireview, pages 114, 116; Flight International, page 92; Alan W. Hall, page 18; Howard Levy, page 28; Karel Masojidek, page 8; Stephen P. Peltz, pages 42, 64, 84, 108, 132, 156, 208, 210, 225; Capt. K. E. Sissons, page 206; Prof. Johannes Zopp, page 218. The three-view silhouettes published in this volume are copyright Pilot Press Limited and may not be reproduced without prior permission.

INDEX OF AIRCRAFT TYPES

Printed for the Publishers by
Butler & Tanner Ltd, Frome and London

1366.1073